The author flying his TWIN COMANCHE named ''GOLDEN BOY'' for the Transatlantic Air Rally.

Challenging the Skies

HORIZONS
AROUND THE WORLD

Happy Landings always!

Don Fonger

by Donald Fonger

ISBN: 0–9693675–0–3

Published by
Challenging The Skies
600 South Drive
Winnipeg, MB R3T 0B1   Canada

First Printing, 1988

Printed and bound in Canada by
Friesen Printers
a Division of D. W. Friesen & Sons Ltd.
Altona, Manitoba
Canada
R0G 0B0

DEDICATION

To my two favorite co-pilots, my sons.

ACKNOWLEDGMENTS

Like our flying, the production of this book has been a family affair. Three people have helped me from start to finish. My son and co-pilot Jim Fonger worked with me on the format and content. My brother, Jack Fonger, and son-in-law, Patrick Bennett, have both proofread and made valuable suggestions toward its final form. I wish to acknowledge their help and support. I wouldn't want to have tackled this volume without them.

I am also indebted to Thomas J. Hope, who helped me learn to use my computer and word processor, on which this book was composed.

PHOTO CREDITS

The photograph of me beside my aeroplane, which is located inside the jacket cover at the back of the book, was taken by Ulo Sepp of St. Jovite, Quebec.

Back jacket cover photo by Norma Fonger.

CONTENTS

GLOSSARY

There are a few abbreviations the non-pilot should be familiar with before reading this book. The main ones are: —

Flight Rules:

VFR – Visual Flight Rules. Not radar controlled. Flown in generally clear weather with reference to the ground. Visibility should be 3 miles or more. Must remain 1 mile clear of cloud horizontally and 500 feet vertically. "See and Be Seen" is the rule.

IFR – Instrument Flight Rules. Usually radar controlled. Flown with reference to the aircraft instruments. Airlines fly IFR in all weather. Private aircraft usually fly IFR in poor or marginal weather.

Navigational Equipment:

VOR – Very High Frequency, Omni–directional Radial. The commonest navigational instrument. Shows pilot where the aircraft is in relation to an imaginary radial line on the ground.

ADF – Automatic Direction Finder. Points directly at the navigational station it is tuned to. Will also point toward commercial broadcast stations. This is sometimes useful. e.g. Commercial station 550 on Maui is stronger than the navigational ADF station in Honolulu and can therefore be received farther out to sea.

DME – Distance Measuring Equipment, Continuously displays distance to the next (or previous) navigational station. Also displays speed actually being made across ground or water. Works to about 100 miles.

LORAN C – Long Range Navigational System — Type C. Originally used for marine navigation. Miniaturization of equipment has made it practical and economical for use in aeroplanes. Provides latitude, longitude, groundspeed and other information but there is no signal south of the equator or in certain other areas around the world.

SAT NAV – Satellite Navigator. Triangulates signals from among approximately 16 satellites to provide latitude and longitude about once every hour. Works all over the world. Not normally installed in small aircraft. Portable models used in ferry flights across the Pacific Ocean because distance are too great for all other navigational signals.

INTRODUCTION

The ultimate experience in the life of a pilot must surely be to circumnavigate the world in his own light aircraft. To perform this feat with his son as co–pilot is indeed a dream come true. Imagine the challenge of flying nonstop across the world's largest ocean in an aeroplane barely large enough to lift the crew and required Pacific–crossing fuel off the ground.

This is the story of how my eldest son and I progressed to that point and what happened when we did!

As long as I can remember, I have always wanted to take off and fly far above the earth and antlike traffic below, but I didn't actually realize my ambition until I was nine years old. My first experience with this wonderful sense of freedom came in the 1930s at the Municipal Airport in Saskatoon, Saskatchewan. Barnstorming pilots, flying biplanes, had come to town and were offering rides over the city for one cent per pound. There was one catch however, the minimum price per flight was $2.00. I convinced my brother to come with me and he and I, in our winter coats, weighed just under two hundred pounds. So up we went, side by side in the passenger seat, and the seed was sown: *I would learn to fly someday.*

No member of my own family, nor any of my friends were particularly interested in flying so I contented myself for the next several years building model aeroplanes. I spent many a pleasant hour in my adolescent years cutting out wing spars from balsa wood and cutting and gluing balsa wood sticks into truss–shaped fuselages. I covered the assembled frames with special thin paper which was then shrunk tight with banana oil. Model aeroplanes were powered in those days by elastic bands twisted to unwind and turn the propellor for an all too short flight.

When I was just entering my teens I had the misfortune to break my arm in several places and had gone on to develop an infection in the bone. Fortunately I successfully fought off the infection by myself without the help of Sulfa and Penicillin, which were not yet in general use. Little did I realize at the time how this accident would resurface to affect my chances of flying.

In 1939, when war broke out, I could see how my wish to become a pilot might at last be realized. As soon as I turned eighteen, I applied to join the Royal Canadian Air Force as air crew. My fondest dreams turned to ashes when the medical staff decided that the osteomyelitis infection, caused by those broken bones piercing the skin and entering the dirt six years before, might come back. The army medical staff were not as particular and I found myself in the Royal Canadian Armoured Corps instead. The only flights I could manage during my three years in military service were two circuits in Harvard (T–6 in the U.S.) trainers, courtesy of some friends in the R.C.A.F. This was enough to convince me that the urge to fly was still in my blood.

It was not until my discharge from the army in January 1946, when I entered university, that I was at last to realize my heart's desire. To my astonishment and delight, I found that some Air Force veterans at the university had formed a University Flying Club. They had also convinced the Student's Union to purchase them a brand new 1946 Taylorcraft BC 12D fabric covered aeroplane, complete with a 65 H.P. engine. There were no such luxuries as a radio or an electric starter but it was beautiful! At last, here was my opportunity.

My tuition and a small allowance toward a meagre personal existence were being paid by the veterans department of the government, but there was no money left over for flying lessons. The only solution was to get a part time job. I found a job marking math assignments for one of the professors and began saving the proceeds in a shoe box marked "Flying lessons". When I had accumulated $100.00 I immediately joined the flying club and started my instruction. The ground school text was called "From The Ground

Up'' and cost $1.00. The flying lessons, with an instructor on board cost $6.00 per hour. The cost of flying Solo, when I reached that degree of proficiency, was $5.00 per hour.

Since it was during the winter, my training was on the aircraft equipped with skis instead of wheels. When I lifted that Taylorcraft free of its earthly bonds for the first time I was exhilarated, but I couldn't help but wonder what held the whole thing together. All I could see around me in the cockpit were a few bars of light metal tubing and some fabric covering, reminding me of my balsa wood models. The whole thing just didn't look strong enough to do the job. My early landings proved to me that it was, in fact, a stout little plane, and by the summer I had amassed the impressive sum of three hours. I had also begun to believe that all those instruments on the panel might eventually be coordinated by one individual.

The next fall I resumed my training, and in May 1948 I wrote the written exam without any formal ground school. In the same month, with a total time of twenty-two hours, I passed my private licence. In addition to the total cost of $150.00, which included the medical examination costs, there were two major differences that will be difficult for today's students to understand. *No cross country flight experience was required and the examiner never got into the aeroplane during the flight test. He simply sat in a chair beside the runway and graded you, while looking up from the ground.*

Following a walk-around and a number of questions, posed by the flight examiner, I got into the aircraft alone and flew around the airport, climbing until I reached 5000 feet. The test consisted of putting the plane into a spin to the right and falling three full turns, leveling off at 4000 feet. As soon as the plane was under control, another spin was required in the opposite direction for three more full turns, pulling out at around 3000 feet. From this point, the next exercise was to make a forced landing on the airport without using the engine, except to clear it briefly every thousand feet. I was required to come to a natural rolling stop, without using the brakes, within one hundred feet of a flag the examiner had placed near the middle of the grass runway. I flew all of this successfully, and after two more consecutive, rolling-stop landings near the flag, I was a Private Pilot — *But Still Without Any Cross Country Experience!*

1

Progressive Challenges

THE FIRST CROSS COUNTRY

Like the initial Solo, the first cross country flight holds special memories. I had learned that all Private licenses obtained before 1949 were going to have to be upgraded by making a triangular flight to two other airports (each at least sixty miles apart and from the airport of origin.) Arrival at each airport was to be certified by having the controller in the tower sign the log upon landing. I chose my airports and went to my instructors for help in organizing my flight. It was decided that I could make the flight using only my compass, a map and "rules of thumb" for correcting wind drift.

It was possible to make the flight by following the rivers and railroads, but with beginner's zeal, I elected to attempt to fly direct. The only problem with this plan was that the flight was to take place in the province of New Brunswick, Canada, and the direct lines between the selected airports were all over uninhabited forest.

On May 4, 1949 I rented my favorite Taylorcraft and took off across the bush on the first leg of my triangular flight, from Fredericton to Moncton, New Brunswick. It was a beautiful, clear, cool spring day and I was anxiously anticipating this new adventure. Pilot training today always includes one cross country flight with an instructor before heading off on your own. However, in 1949 it was common to do it "cold turkey." After all in the year since I obtained my license, I had amassed another 5 1/2 hours flying time, including checkouts on two additional types of aircraft, the Aeronca and the Tiger Moth. Like the early R.A.F. pilots of W.W.II, I was almost over-qualified for the trip!

Everything went well at first. I was flying along about 2,000 feet above the thick forest when suddenly my engine began to run very rough. **It sputtered and coughed, and I was sure it was going to quit altogether.** The old pilots' saying that "Flying is 98% being bored to tears and 2% being scared to death" flashed through my mind. This seemed a little early in my career for the 2% to be surfacing. I fought back the nauseous feeling of panic and scanned the cockpit at my meagre assortment of instruments. I could spot nothing wrong! *The nearest possible place to put the plane down was several miles off to my right, where the trees had been cleared along the sides of a river. I instinctively turned towards the river.*

I found out later, there were apparently two possible solutions to my predicament. All I could think of at the time was to shove in the throttle to obtain whatever power was still available and climb as high as possible, before the engine quit altogether and I was forced to land. Hopefully, I would be alongside the river by then!

I learned later that carburetor icing was the culprit. The correct solution was to have pulled out the lever which turns on the carburetor heat and wait while the engine first runs even rougher (while the ice in the carburetor melts into water and passes through the engine) and then returns to normal smooth operation. I had used carburetor heat every time I cut back on power during all my winter training flights, but unfortunately, no one had ever told me that aeroplane engines could ice up on such a deceptively beautiful, yet deceitful, Spring day.

Needless to say, my fearless approach to this first cross country flight had melted along with the ice, and I flew the remainder of all three legs in close proximity to either the river or a road. I also resolved that, from now on, all my flying would be done in the SAFEST way possible under any given set of circumstances. Flying will always have some inherent risk. The secret, I decided, was in completing enough study and training to minimize the risk.

Another lesson I learned on this flight was that it is not necessary to land a small two-seater aeroplane on the first one hundred feet of a 10,000 foot long runway, particularly when your first exit is somewhere near the middle. I knew that my novice rank must have shown by the smiles I received from the tower controllers, when I requested my checkpoint validating signature from them.

From Moncton, this first cross country excursion took me to St. John and back to Fredericton. The return flight to Fredericton was without further incident and my private license was now ready for the upcoming new government regulations.

25 YEARS LATER – 1974

Now let's move ahead in time twenty-five years to meet the family and learn of two more firsts in cross country flight. The major credit for our flying family belongs to my wife, Vivienne. She has never become addicted to flying in small aeroplanes but is a willing passenger as long as she approves of the proposed destination. Vivienne is also perhaps our most relaxed passenger. Several times I have noticed her sound asleep while the aircraft is still taxiing to the active runway for takeoff.

Our eldest child, Jim, is currently a practicing heart surgeon in Boston, Massachusetts. Because of his early interest in flying, he has been my co-pilot on the majority of my cross country flights.

Next eldest is my daughter, Norma. Despite taking the five hour co-pilot orientation course, she had no desire to go further with her flight training. She has never hesitated to be a passenger, however, as long as the initial flight from home is farther south into warmer weather. Our youngest, Bob, became a flying instructor after high school. When he realized, in the early 1980's that opportunities with the airlines were virtually non-existent, he went back to school and took Business Administration. He now manages a local electronics distributorship.

After my first cross country experience, I went on to graduate in Civil Engineering and completed a year of post graduate study in London, England. Upon returning to Canada I have spent all my working years as a general contractor. Neither of my sons or myself are employed as professional pilots. However, we have all taken further instruction to obtain commercial licenses with multi-engine and instrument ratings. This additional training has served us well in some of our more adventurous subsequent flights.

Now back to the firsts in cross country flights I promised. When Jim obtained his private license, he had about forty hours of total flight time. I owned a two-seater Cessna 150 at the time. Seven days after he obtained his license, we flew 120 nautical miles to Grand Forks, North Dakota. This accomplished two important objectives. The first was to learn the procedures for crossing a border by air and learning to deal with foreign controllers, weather briefers and customs authorities. The second was to practice flying straight and level and then making a 180 degree turn around while wearing a hood. This exercise would simulate the action required by a pair of non-instrument rated pilots, such as ourselves, should we enter a cloud by mistake. We felt this was likely to happen sometime during the bold undertaking we had in mind for the following week.

Our plan was to double Jim's flying hours and give him some practical cross country flying experience by flying our little Cessna 150 from Canada to the Mexican border and back. We had hoped for a six day round trip flight, which meant we would have to fly between 600 and 800 statute miles per day. We planned to visit Jim's grandparents in Tucson, Arizona, for two days rest at the midway point.

The main reason we chose this route and destination for our first major cross country flight was a chart we had discovered, in an aviation publication, showing that the entire trip had better than an 80% statistical chance of being flown under visual flight rules during daylight hours in winter.

We soon discovered that 80% is a large 20% short of perfect! It was twenty-seven degrees below zero when we departed on December 13th and we flew only as far as Valley City, North Dakota before encountering a snow storm. Jim made the 180 degree turn he had practiced and diverted to clearer weather at Fargo, North Dakota. Reluctantly we both bought bathing suits and spent the next day and a half around the hotel pool. We then flew as far as Grand Island, Nebraska in the clear and ran into cloud once again.

The First Cross Country

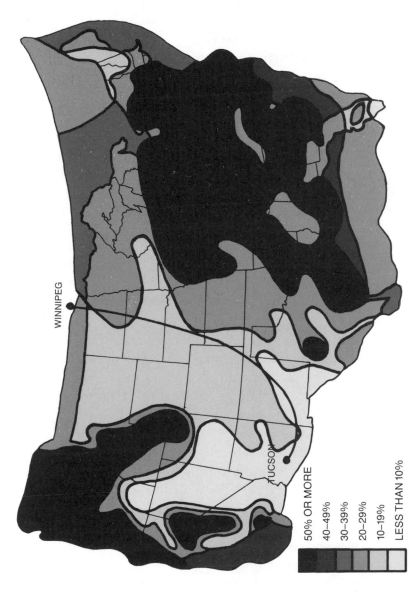

WINNIPEG

TUCSON

50% OR MORE
40–49%
30–39%
20–29%
10–19%
LESS THAN 10%

Maximum percentage of hours during any one month in winter when the ceiling is below VFR limits.

Our diversion this time was to Hutchinson, Kansas, a few miles north west of Wichita, for the night.

The next morning, strong headwinds forced us to abandon Lubbock, Texas, as our first destination of the day, and opt for a closer alternate at Childress. We landed on a seldom used runway surrounded by cotton fields. There was no one in the hangar, but a note suggested we try contacting the owner on the office radio. He was out crop dusting in his aeroplane. We did this and a friendly voice told us where to turn on the electricity, gave us permission to take whatever gas we required, and asked us to leave fifty-two cents per gallon on his office desk. *We never met our helpful host but certainly comment him for his friendly attitude toward other pilots needing help.*

The following morning, the 80% clear stretch of VFR weather we were expecting from our chart finally materialized. The early morning is clearly the best time to fly and we were off the ground before 8:00 AM. Our gas stops included Carlsbad, New Mexico, and El Paso, Texas. Seventy miles west of El Paso we came upon the towns of Columbus, New Mexico, and Puerto Palomas, Mexico, about a mile apart. To achieve the trip objective of reaching Mexico, we dipped south briefly and straddled the Mexican border before heading north west again to Tucson.

Although there was a lower and longer route from there to Tucson, we elected to fly the more direct airway which included an 8,000 foot ridge. The recommended method of crossing a high mountain ridge in a small plane is to climb to an altitude at least 2,000 feet higher than the crest and then cross it at a forty-five degree angle. This allows for a quick reversal should you encounter a severe downdraft just before reaching the ridge. The little Cessna 150 had its work cut out reaching 10,000 feet in hot weather at gross weight. Finally, at 10,100 feet, which was clearly the ceiling for our little plane, we approached the ridge and immediately dropped 400 feet while still pointed upwards with the throttle wide open. *One further downdraft and we would have had to abandon the ridge crossing and go the long way around.* Jim waited on the controls, poised for action, but soon we were over the top and headed down the other side into Tucson. That was it! It was now clear to us why a substantial safety margin is recommended in this situation. We had learned yet another lesson of how you can minimize risk in flight.

Two days later, it was time to leave Tucson for home, since we had promised faithfully to be back before Christmas. When we checked the weather on the morning of December 19th, we learned the next hard cross–country lesson. The wind had switched and would also be a headwind on the way home. At an average ground speed of only eighty–five miles per hour, it had taken over twenty–four flying hours bucking head winds on the trip to Tucson. We didn't do much better on the way back. Unfortunately, much to our chagrin, we averaged only ninety miles per hour ground speed and sat huddled together in those confined quarters for another twenty–one hours on the way home. However, Jim had more than doubled his flying hours in only nine days. In that short time he had learned a great deal about aircraft performance, map reading, electronic navigation, radio work and the uncertainties of weather for the VFR pilot. That was not bad for his first real cross country flight!

4 YEARS LATER – 1978

Bob finished high school in 1978 and started taking flying lessons with a plan for a career in aviation. Soon it was his turn to bring home that prized piece of paper – his Private Pilot's License. It wasn't many days after that when he casually asked "Well, dad, when do we go?" History was repeating itself within our own family! I didn't have to be told what he meant.

A few days later, we were off again to Grand Forks, North Dakota, to practice the same procedures I had done with Jim and to start making plans for another sojourn south. We had no one to visit in Tucson that year, but we did have good friends wintering in McAllen, Texas, on the Mexican border, so that would be our destination.

Eight days later, after another thirty–nine hours huddled in the cramped right hand seat of that Cessna 150, I was back home again. Following many of the same experiences as on our first trip south, we now had a third qualified pilot in the family, complete with some real cross country flight time.

Bob also found romance in the skies. When he later spent a spell as a flight instructor, he taught a number of young women the intricacies of handling an aeroplane in the sky. One particular petite brunette student named Sharon caught his fancy and his spirits soared to new heights. She later brought him down to earth with a walk down the long church aisle. Today, although Sharon no longer exercises her pilot's license very often, she successfully co-pilots Bob through the turbulence of a rough business world as his devoted wife and my daughter-in-law.

OUTSIDE THE FAMILY

I like this picture so much, I just had to include the story about the duck that ended his career on a cross country flight of his own.

Spring and Fall Hazard for both Ducks and Pilots.

In the springtime, ducks crowd the flyways northward through the U.S. and Canada heading for their summer breeding grounds. A local pilot, on his first solo cross country flight, inadvertently flew into a flock of ducks about 100 miles from where the aircraft was based. There was a ''thud'' somewhere up front, but the aircraft had no visible damage and still flew as it should. Nervously, the novice pilot landed at the nearest airport and discovered a dead duck wedged into his front cowling. Somehow this duck had flown through the spinning propellor without hitting it, much as the machine gun bullets were fired through the propellors of some fighter aircraft during the 1914 – 1918 war.

He was hesitant to remove the duck because he thought the rushing air in flight would tear the frail cowling apart. *He left the bird where it was and flew home safely with the duck's head swinging like a pendulum in the breeze.* That pilot will always remember **his** first cross–country flight!

2

Progressive Challenges

MOVING UP

By 1974, the two seater Cessna 150 had become too small for the family and too slow for me to use in visiting my distant construction sites. I bought a new four place Cessna 172, added a package of King radios suitable for instrument flight, and Jim and I commenced upgrading our flying skills. Soon we both had commercial licenses and single-engine instrument ratings. We were now ready to expand our horizons once again.

A flight to The Bahamas seemed like a natural progression of our experience. We found the addresses of various accommodations for rent throughout the Bahamas in a flying magazine and selected Treasure Cay on the island of Great Abaco for a family Christmas vacation. Our space problems were still not completely solved, because we now had four seats available to transport five family members and their considerable baggage. The solution lay in sending my wife, Vivienne, and daughter, Norma, by airline to Freeport, Bahamas, while Bob, Jim and I took most of the baggage with us in the Cessna 172. After landing at Treasure Cay, we emptied the plane and I returned to Freeport for the ladies.

Our preliminary plans for the flight included three possible routes between Winnipeg and West Palm Beach. The direct line went through areas of probable unsuitable weather. Our second choice was drawn as a gentle arc west of the direct route. The surest bet for good weather en route was a third course directly south through Kansas City and Little Rock, Arkansas, then heading southeast into Florida via Montgomery, Alabama. We would let the actual weather on the day of the flight dictate the route. I have made this flight from Canada several times now. Each time, it has proved best to travel the extra distance and fly the most westerly route in more stable weather. To make certain that the ladies wouldn't be kept waiting for us, we allowed two days to get to West Palm from Winnipeg.

We started our trip early in the morning and planned for the longest leg first, while we were fresh. With three pilots, we were able to stretch our flying hours and reached Orlando, Florida, that night. As a reward for our long flight, we spent the next day at Disneyworld while we waited for the jet carrying the ladies to catch up with us.

The following morning, we made the short hop to West Palm Beach and prepared for our first overwater flight. Normally, single engine aeroplanes are not permitted to fly over water any farther than they could glide if their engine were to fail. There are special regulations for the Bahamas, however, because distances are moderate and communications are good. I suppose the fact that the water is warm is also a factor, as it gives downed fliers a reasonable chance of staying alive until they are rescued. All the required survival equipment can be rented at the West Palm Beach airport, but we had brought our own. We filed an oceanic flight plan, brought the life raft up into the front seat, stuffed the shark repellant into our pockets and departed for Treasure Cay.

The first flight out over the ocean, when sight of land is lost, gives one a very strange and lonely feeling. Many people do this every day, and the aircraft engine has never quit before – so there is no good reason for it to do so now. However, regardless of all this logic, as soon as sight of land is lost, the engine starts to sound different. This phenomenon is well known to seasoned pilots and is sometimes referred to as ''Automatic Rough.'' Fortunately it is usually all in the pilot's mind.

Once we were used to the solitude of ocean flying, it was time to look for our first landfall. Even when the sky is clear over the water, there is usually a cloud around the islands. When in doubt – fly toward the low clouds – there is likely land underneath. Our radio navigation was working well, and we soon had the family safely on the ground for Christmas at Treasure Cay.

Four Fongers on Scuba Dive at Freeport, Bahamas. Jim, Norma, Don, Bob.

After Christmas, the three children and myself flew back to Freeport for a day of beginners' scuba diving. Following three hours of instruction, we were taken out with a group to the reefs and made our dives under the watchful eye of an instructor. It was a wonderful experience in this clear, warm water, and I decided then and there that this was something else for which I would have to obtain my ticket. One of the other divers took our family photo and sent it to us after we got home. That was fortunate, for we have never all been together under water since. As beginning divers, none of our dives were very deep. This prevented the necessity of staying on the ground, awaiting full decompression of our bodies, before flying back to Treasure Cay at altitude.

By December 30th, the ladies began to talk of shopping, so the next morning we left Bob at our condominium with a promise to return before dark, and Jim and I flew the women to Nassau for a day in the stores. A couple of hours before sunset, we returned to the plane and left for home. We were flight planned for 6500 feet, but as we climbed through five thousand feet, the engine suddenly started banging and backfiring with frightening implications. Jim was flying, and I had been leaning the fuel mixture for him as we climbed. I immediately returned the mixture to full rich, but that was not the problem. I then hurriedly checked the position of the fuel selector valve, but it was correct. Nassau was behind us on the horizon, and Jim instinctively started turning in that direction. The ladies in back of us had been carrying their life jackets on their laps. They were now donning them as fast as they could! I remember thinking that we would probably get out of this mess somehow – for the Caribbean water below us was warm enough to be survivable. I did wonder, however, if we could survive long enough for a search party to rescue us. After all, it was New Year's Eve and they might not be able to get a search party together for two or three days!

Jim and I decided to try the magneto switches. He switched one off and there was dead silence. I don't think I can ever remember anything more quiet. Jim hurriedly turned the switch back on again and the engine came back to life, but it was still bucking and banging. We were losing altitude far too fast to make it back to the island. Then Jim turned off the other magneto switch, and the engine smoothed out immediately. Now we had time to answer the questions that were coming from the back seats. We explained that we had just lost one of our electrical ignition systems, but, fortunately, all aircraft have two complete sets of spark plugs in every cylinder and two magnetos feeding them, just in case this very thing happens.

Jim advised the tower at Nassau of our problem, and we returned safely for repairs. The mechanics were capable and cooperative. A couple of hours later they had rebuilt the faulty magneto, and the plane was ready again for flight. There was, however, one problem remaining. It was now too dark to fly home. (VFR flight is prohibited in the Bahamas after sunset and the runway at Treasure Cay is without lights and is not equipped for instrument landings.) It was also New Year's Eve. Bob was alone back at Treasure Cay with a whole condominium to himself, but no phone. We were in Nassau for the night with no overnight attire, but clothing didn't appear to be our most immediate problem.

There were no hotel rooms available anywhere in Nassau, that we could find.

3 sets of Bare Legs spend a Formal New Year's Eve in Nassau, following a Magneto failure. Jim, Don, Norma, Vivienne.

Eventually one of the locals, attempting to help us with our problem, contacted an exclusive country club on the island and talked them into letting us occupy two guest rooms they had vacant. We were quick to accept and checked in. We hadn't eaten since lunch, and the only meal at the club was the formal New Year's Eve dinner in the main dining room. The maitre d' felt sorry for us and seated us at a table in the corner of the room, out of the way and out of sight as much as possible. We all covered our bare legs with their large white linen napkins and tried to look as inconspicuous as possible. No matter how hard we tried – we just didn't look right. Everyone else was in Tuxedos and long formal evening gowns.

The maitre d' returned and apologetically explained that a number of the guests were complaining about all the money that they were spending on this evening, only to have the whole atmosphere ruined by the odd looking group in the corner. He moved us into a small staff room and served us the same meal as the $100.00 guests. We called the main lodge back at Treasure Cay and asked them to deliver a message to where Bob was staying, telling him that we were all right and that he would be alone for the night. They agreed to advise him, but Bob never got the message. *He spent a very anxious night wondering about the other four fifths of his family.*

In the morning we checked out early, before the office staff had recovered from New Year's Eve and opened up the main supply of cash. Our bill came to $105.00 and I paid with two $100.00 travellers cheques. The only change available at this hour was in one dollar bills, so I stuffed my change, a roll of ninety-five of them, into the pockets of my short pants, and we headed back to put Bob's mind at rest. The aircraft magneto worked well, and as far as I know, has never given any more trouble to this day.

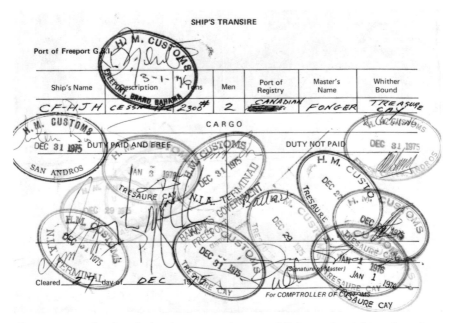

Customs paper for aircraft showing many trips around Bahamas for sight-seeing, shopping and scuba diving.

Before leaving for home, we made several other local trips between the islands. One of our very pleasant trips was a flight to the most northerly island in the Bahamas, Walker Cay, for lunch and a stroll around their popular marina. Private aircraft in the Bahamas provide a lot of utility. There is no better "taxi" for touring the many friendly islands.

The trip home a few days later, was straightforward, but as usual, contained some bad weather. Following our first night's stop at Tallahassee, Florida, we awakened to a morning of pouring rain. The weather briefer informed us that the rain should only bother us for about 100 miles and then it would be clear all the way to Canada. If we had not had an instrument-rated pilot along we might have spent several days waiting for that front to pass. Jim volunteered to take us out of the rain and flight planned for 6,000 feet. We were cruising along on autopilot when the controller advised that he had a pilot report stating there was no rain in this area at 8,000 feet and offered us that altitude. Since we only had a few miles left to fly in this rain, Jim advised the controller that we were comfortable where we were and that this might be our last chance to wash the aircraft before we returned to the frozen north. "Thanks anyway." I feel certain that there was a smile on that controller's face as we flew northward out of his sector.

A year later, Jim, Bob, and I flew a similar route to Florida again, this time to the Florida Keys to scuba dive. We all had our diving certification cards by now. Bob wanted to build up his flying hours on this trip – so we let him. I have never had it so easy. I sat in the back seat all the way to Miami and slept.

We dove out of Key Largo, Florida. On our first dive, we visited an underwater statue of Christ, standing with his arms outstretched toward the filtered sunlight above. The figure was anchored there, beneath the surface, to look after all those who have lost their life at sea in this area. I understand it was copied from a similar underwater statue in the Bay of Naples, Italy.

The second dive was made among a series of rocky under-water corridors to visit the divemaster's friendly six foot electric Moray eel. We were instructed to swim along the bottom in a certain direction until we came to two discarded car batteries. Then we were to turn left for one hundred yards to a large rock. The eel lived under the far side of this rock. Somehow, when we arrived at the rock, Jim got turned around. He was right in front of the eel's hiding place and didn't know it. The eel knew it though, and he came out and headed straight for Jim. Normally quite dangerous, this large eel was used to being fed by divers and was simply looking for food. Suddenly, Jim saw him about one foot away. Startled, Jim beat a hasty retreat. *I have never seen a diver travel backwards under water with such agility! If Bob and I hadn't had air regulators in our mouths, we would have laughed out loud.*

Since we were returning before the end of Christmas holidays, Jim wanted to stop for a few days of skiing at Vail, Colorado. Bob took off from Miami International and flew all day and all night to Denver, with me asleep again most of the time in the back. I don't ever remember a clearer night for flying. Even map reading was possible in the bright moonlight. Bob entered 16 hours in his log book that day and went to bed for a well deserved rest. The next day we said "Good-bye" to Jim, and Bob flew me home. His horizons had opened up considerably.

3

Progressive Challenges

THE COMMERCIAL PERIOD

A local radio station offered a Honda Civic car as their prize for whoever could make the biggest and best sign saying that they were the Number One radio station. Jim and a friend took up the challenge. One contestant spelled out the message using bales of hay arranged on the side of a hill. Another ploughed the letters into his farm field. Jim's approach was different.

He had heard that there was a box of unused aerial banner letters stored somewhere at the airport. He eventually located them and found a single letter-size sheet of instructions containing a brief description on how to pick up banners from the air and fly them. There was no number one in the ancient kit, and he knew he couldn't win using any other number, so he made one. He then had to learn the art of banner flying, basically by trial and error.

The aeroplane does not take off with the letters attached. It would never get off the ground or reach flying speed, dragging that long banner down the runway. The aircraft is fitted with a rope that has a three-pronged metal grappling hook at one end and a loop at the other. The loop is secured to the tail of the plane with a catch that can be released from inside the cockpit. The pilot takes off with his left hand out through an open window, holding onto the free end of the rope by the metal hook. *After he is airborne, he casts the hook out and it trails down behind the plane on its rope at roughly forty-five degrees.*

An assistant on the ground has put up two poles and strung the banner rope between them to form a "clothes line." The pilot then swoops down toward the suspended line and attempts to catch it with the dangling hook as he passes. *If he is successful, he then climbs at full power and lifts the banner from the ground, much as one peels a banana skin from a banana.* Once the banner is in the air, the flight is conducted right at the stall speed of the aircraft. The aircraft can't stall and spin however, because in order to allow a wing to drop and the nose to turn, the tail must move in the opposite direction. The banner fixes the tail position and won't allow this to happen. Stalling therefore results in a gentle "mush" and doesn't progress into a spin.

To jettison the banner, the pilot flies over the field, just to the side of the runway and pulls a cord to release the tail hook. The banner and the rope with the hook on it all fall clear of the aircraft, and the pilot is free to land and attach the hook again in preparation for the next banner.

Jim gradually mastered this technique by trial and error on a grass strip and arranged to fly his contest banner for the judges while they attended a professional football game. Not only did he and his friend win the car, but he started to receive calls from companies wanting their messages flown at succeeding games. After all, there was a guaranteed captive audience of 30,000 plus people, mostly adults, sitting there with nothing to look at but a green field or blue sky between plays. His part-time business was born.

For the next few years, he supplemented his income, while attending medical school, with revenue from flying banners. He also persuaded the Number One radio station into starting an aerial Traffic Watch broadcast, helping automobile traffic out of, and back into, the city on Friday and Sunday evenings. Several times, when he wanted a night off for a special event, I flew his banners for him, but he never let me do his radio broadcasts. He always insisted that my voice was too old for the youthful audience of the radio station for which he was working.

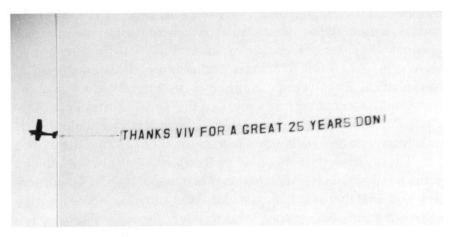

THANKS VIV FOR A GREAT 25 YEARS DON!

World's largest 25th Anniversary Card.

In return for helping him out with the banner flying, Jim provided me with a customized banner for my own use on a very special occasion. On my twenty-fifth wedding anniversary I flew my wife's anniversary card instead of mailing it. Fortunately, the big day happened to coincide with a home game of our professional football team. Some friends arranged to take my wife, Vivienne, to the game with them. I claimed I had to help Jim fly some banners during the first half. There was also a seat at the stadium for me, and I agreed to join them during the intermission and sit with them for the last half of the game.

After my first two banners were flown,the ground crew laid out my anniversary card in the grass beside the runway. I dove for the field, hooked the banner and headed for the stadium. Everyone except Vivienne in the surrounding seats knew what was going to happen. *She got the surprise of her life when she saw her name and mine being towed around in front of thirty thousand people! I circled the stadium three times and returned to the airport. Just as the second half started, I arrived to proudly take my seat beside her. The spectators for rows around us clapped and cheered – and not for the football game. All the world loves a romantic!*

When Jim graduated from Medicine, he left home to do his intern year and surgery residency in Toronto. A young friend of his, Ron Renz, was studying engineering at the university here and was also keen on flying. I let him fly my aircraft to build the hours he required for his commercial license. He obtained his commercial license just as it was time for Jim to leave. Ron took over the banner flying and the traffic watch for the radio station, for his final two years in school here, and then it was time for him to leave also. Ron went to Kansas and continued his education in Aeronautical Engineering. Neither of us knew it then, but he would return my favor many fold in a few years. Ron later became my main source for aeronautical engineering advice when I ultimately took up the challenge of planning a flight around the world.

The business didn't stop when Ron left town either. We called in the family reserves. My son Bob had now obtained his commercial and instructor's licenses. He was earning some money instructing but, as everyone who has ever instructed knows, not nearly enough. He was anxious to fly the banners and become a weekend airborne radio announcer. So, for two years he carried on the tradition faithfully – even to refusing to allow me to talk on that radio station. It was time for me to show my two sons that I was not as old as they seemed to think.

I DECIDED TO TAKE UP SKY DIVING!

There was a one day course at the airport in Pembina, North Dakota. It consisted of eight hours of instruction and culminated with a first jump. All this was included in one package price. One Saturday I joined the group and was surprised to see just how young the other jumpers were. They convinced me that there were lots of people my age jumping regularly, so I paid my money and continued.

At the end of the day, the weather deteriorated before all of our class had jumped, so my jump was scheduled for the next day. I was able to talk my wife and daughter into driving to Pembina with me the next morning to witness the family breadwinner proving he could do something the boys couldn't, or rather wouldn't, do. I suited up as shown in the picture, complete with chutes front and back, a crash helmet, gloves and boots. *I was completely protected – as long as the chute opened.*

Our jump plane was a Cessna 180. It contained a pilot, a jumpmaster and two first time jumpers. At 2,800 feet above the ground the jumpmaster dropped a wooden stick, with a ribbon attached, directly over the target landing area. The stick drops at the same rate as a person in a parachute. The jumpmaster can tell

The author dressed for his first (and last) Skydive.

from where it lands, how far upwind the student jumper should jump so as to land in the desired area. I was the closest to the door so I got to go first. I crawled out of the plane and stood on the little step they had attached to the right wheel for this purpose. *We had been told that no one is permitted to re–enter the plane once they have climbed outside of the cabin. It is too dangerous. The parachute might catch on something and open accidentally. It would then tear off the side of the aeroplane, with disastrous results for all.*

Even though I knew it was a one way trip, I climbed out as ordered by the jumpmaster. My left foot was on the little step. My right foot was swinging in the breeze and my hands were locked onto the wing strut in a deathlike grip. At the calculated spot, the jumpmaster slapped me on the rear, and I pushed back and entered the spread eagle position, as I had been taught the previous day. *Fortunately, the rules dictate that one's first five jumps are made with the rip cord attached firmly to the aeroplane, so that it is pulled automatically as you fall away. I am not sure that I would have remembered to pull it – I was so busy trying for a perfect spread eagle.*

The jumpmaster had said I should remember to look up as I fell, and tell him how many fingers he was holding out the door. If my spread eagle was correct, and my head was up where it should be, I would be able to see his outstretched hand above me. I never even saw the aeroplane. I was looking at the ground. It seemed to take forever as I fell earthward, tense and alone, waiting for the welcome jerk on my harness. Finally, there it was! My main chute opened and I started to float earthward. It was so quiet without the sound of an aircraft engine in my ears! The jump plane was now in the distance, and there was only the sound of a light rush of wind in my chute. I looked down and saw our little group of well-wishers near the landing area. **THE LANDING AREA!. That's what I should have been concentrating on!** I was drifting away! I pulled on the parachute's steering handles and brought myself around toward the group, but not soon enough. I was not going to land in the soft target circle. I was going to make contact on the hard–baked clay near the runway. Up higher,. I had seemed to be falling quite slowly. As I neared the ground, I could see just how fast I was **really** falling. I brought my legs together and got ready to roll upon contact. **Wham! I hit like a ton of bricks!**

The experienced jumpers in the watching crowd knew that this was not a good landing and came running toward me. One of my ankles was at least severely twisted, and I knew I couldn't walk. *Vivienne, at this point I am sure, was wondering if she could stand another twenty–five years of this nonsense.* She brought our car over beside me, and several of the men hauled me up and into the back seat. They strapped my legs together, to keep them from moving, and my wife and daughter drove me back home to the hospital. The diagnosis was a broken bone in one leg and a badly wrenched ankle on the other. Two weeks in bed, and another two on crutches, and I was nearly as good as new.

One might ask what all this has to do with flying. It certainly was a form of Challenging The Skies. However it also taught me an important lesson. *Never again would I leave a perfectly good aeroplane in the air of my own free will!*

4

Progressive Challenges

ADDING AN ENGINE

The argument about the relative merits of a light twin, versus a single engine aircraft, has been going on for years without a clear winner ever being declared.

There is no doubt that a recreational pilot has very little chance of avoiding a serious crash if one engine on a light twin quits on takeoff near the allowable gross weight. Single engine aircraft will always be more manageable during a high power engine failure. However, once airborne safely, a twin will usually prevent an "engine out" from resulting in an off-airport landing.

I don't think the strongest argument in favor of a single engine aeroplane, is that it will suffer an engine failure only half as often as a twin. I feel the greatest advantage is, that as long as that one engine is running, there will always be cabin heat. The cockpit, with it's engine right in front of the pilot, is heated by ram air forced through the nose. The air passes the hot exhaust manifold, and arrives heated in the cabin. Provided there are no holes in the exhaust system, to allow carbon monoxide as well as heated air into the cabin, the system is simple and therefore dependable.

The twin, however, with its engines out on the wing, makes it impractical to duct the exhaust-heated air into the cabin. The customary solution is to install a separate gasoline–fired heater, either in front of or behind the cabin, and blow the heat around the occupants with an electric fan. This gas heater, unfortunately, is controlled by a number of mechanical and electrical devices, any one of which can fail – and eventually one does. *I can think of at least two bone–chilling experiences I have had while flying in the northern United States and Canada because of this.*

Eventually, my construction endeavors led to bidding for work in Canada's northland. The large lakes in Manitoba made it illegal for me to fly a straight line to the jobsites. I couldn't cross the middle of these vast bodies of water, and still be able to glide to the shore in the event of an engine failure, as required by single engine regulations. It was too far and took too long to go around the lakes in my single engine Cessna. I also needed more room to transport my foremen to sites not served by regional airlines.

My search for a light twin with a good payload, turbocharging, and de–icing equipment, led me to Du Page field in Chicago. There, I located a 6 place Aztec with all of the above features, a good autopilot, and modern avionics. So I entered the multi-engine world, and Jim and I upgraded our licenses and instrument ratings to the standard required for my new aeroplane. Jim flew my men north on Monday mornings. I flew the architect north to inspect the work on Fridays and brought the men home.

One Friday morning, with the architect and an engineer aboard, we were one hour into a two hour cold January flight when the heater quit. At first, this didn't seem to be too serious. We all were wearing warm parkas, the seats and cabin materials were warm, and we only had an hour to go. What we were about to learn was how quickly an aeroplane at 8,000 feet can cool off in January. *The pernicious cold soon crept into the cockpit, and by the time we reached our destination, we were chilled to the very marrow of our bones.*

There was no mechanic at our northern destination, so we were faced with two choices. We could stay where we were and fly a mechanic in Monday or buy extra socks, gloves and underwear and make the trip home travelling a longer route and stopping, to get warm again, at every airport we could find along the way. We chose the latter and visited several new communities on the way home.

One Christmas we decided to visit Cozumel, Mexico, for our vacation. It was reported to have both sunshine for the ladies and scuba diving for the men. With our larger aeroplane, we could now take all five family members. We could also travel farther, faster and higher, than we could before. It seemed logical to push further afield for this holiday and challenge the Mexican skies.

It was on this trip, that I was subjected to my second heater "flame out". When the heat stopped, the cold, clammy, realization occurred to me that the nearest airport on our route, with a service facility, was about thirty minutes away. We took a family vote. It was unanimously agreed that we would be all right for half an hour. There was no point in landing somewhere where they couldn't fix the heater. The outside air was 30 degrees below zero, and the temperature inside the plane plummeted mercilessly. Within fifteen minutes, we were rubbing each other's feet in an attempt to help the circulation in our hands and feet. Jim and I were clapping our hands and stomping our feet up front. The two pilots everyone else was depending on were functioning well below par for the last ten minutes of that flight. Our passengers were so cold when we landed that they had tears in their eyes. *The rapid cooling of an unheated, thin-skinned aeroplane, travelling two hundred miles per hour in sub-zero weather, should not be underestimated!*

We arrived at Cozumel, on the Yucatan peninsula of Mexico, just after dark. Our valid approach plate showed the tower situated in the "V" between the two runways. None of the lights we saw ahead corresponded with the information on our charts. When we finally sorted it all out and landed, we discovered they had built a new tower off to the side and had not yet amended their airport diagrams.

It was December twenty fourth, around seven thirty in the evening, when we entered the terminal and approached the combined customs and immigration officer. He was pleasant and quickly offered me five blank Mexican travel permits for our family to fill out. I returned them and gave him the five we had completed at home before we left. He looked disappointed but stamped them and half-heatedly held them out toward me. *"You understand," he said, "there is absolutely no charge for my services in stamping these papers for you. But after all, sir, IT IS CHRISTMAS EVE!"*

The following day we learned that there was a DC 3 sunk in forty feet of water, about one hundred yards off shore from one of the hotels in Cozumel. This had been done to film a Mexican–American sequel to a movie called "Survive." The original movie told the true story of a soccer team forced down in the Andes mountains and how they were eventually driven to eat the flesh of their dead companions to stay alive. The sequel, being filmed in Cozumel, was the story of a group who were forced to ditch their aeroplane in the water near the shore of a deserted island. The aeroplane was originally positioned close to shore, in shallow water, so that the colors would photograph properly without artificial lights. After the movie was finished, however, a day of rough seas washed the plane farther out to sea and over the edge of a thirty foot underwater precipice. It turned over as it fell and remained in this inverted position four months later when we arrived in Cozumel.

My sons and I went diving on this aircraft wreck. I had never been in the cockpit of a DC 3 before. We had to watch out for each other's air lines inside the aeroplane, for there were a number of places where we could have become snagged. A DC 3 has two airspeed pitot heads under their wings. This DC3 now has none. My two agile co–pilots beat me to them, and I had to settle for a scrap of broken aluminum, I found in the sand beneath the plane, for my souvenir. I had never been in the front cabin of a DC 3 before. In this instance my first visit to the cockpit of the venerable aircraft really involved "Challenging The Seas."

We ran into a trans–border booby trap on the way home. The regulations stated that we had to turn in our tourist cards at our last stop before leaving Mexico. Just before entering the United States, we landed at the border town of Nuevo Laredo. The ceilings in the area that day were only seven hundred feet, so we landed on instruments. I surrendered our cards according to regulation and asked for another instrument flight plan to Laredo – just over the river, on the American side. They suggested that we would be better to cross using a special VFR flight plan, as the distance was very short for an instrument takeoff, hand–off and approach. This made sense to me. I was told to get my clearance from Houston Control while in the air, but as we walked out to the plane to depart, I was called back to the phone. The Mexican controller now advised me that he had obtained the necessary clearance for our special VFR flight from the tower across the river. I confirmed that he had also notified the American customs and took off.

Five minutes later, we landed on the U.S. side in Laredo and asked the ground control , by radio, where to go for customs. The controller told me to park in the yellow circle in front of the tower. He said we could get out of the plane if we wished but not to put a foot outside that yellow circle. In a few minutes, the customs and immigration authorities came out and cleared us. Then, another man approached with a statute book in his hand and informed us that we had just landed in the U.S. without giving any notice, and the fine was Five Hundred Dollars! When I asked if the Mexicans had complied with my request to forward customs notification, he said they had not. He then produced a copy of a book given to U.S. pilots warning them of this booby trap. The book further suggested that pilots should contact the FAA themselves before entering the U.S. and not leave it to anyone else, regardless of what they are told.

The problem, it was finally determined, lay with who owned and staffed the airport. This was not a Federal facility. It was owned and operated by the City of Laredo. The civic employees in the control tower had not passed our arrival information on to the Federal authorities downstairs in Customs and Immigration.

After considerable discussion, I was permitted to type out my own statement explaining how the Mexicans had failed to forward my flight plan to the proper authorities. I was also told to emphasize the fact that none of us spoke or understood Spanish. The fine was miraculously reduced to twenty five dollars, due to the mitigating circumstances. I got the feeling this happened there quite often. *Since I had been prepared to pay the usual twenty five dollars for customs clearance on a Sunday anyway, and since Sunday customs charges had been dropped by the FAA effective January 1st (the day before), I figured I had broken even – and learned another lesson about international flight.*

The increased complexity and performance of our twin engine plane permitted us to fly at altitudes not before possible in its predecessor, the Cessna 172. This brings to mind one trip south with our entire family on board. As we crossed the mountains on the way to California, we climbed up to clear the rocks and got out the oxygen bottle and masks. Climbing through 12,000 feet, we noticed a new problem. Four masks had always been enough for our previous aeroplane. This time, we had two extra seats, and one of these was occupied. There were now five of us, and no one would volunteer not to breathe.

The three most important factors determining one's need for oxygen at any given altitude are age, weight and whether or not a person smokes. An old, fat, smoker requires oxygen at a much lower altitude than a lean youth who never succumbed to the peer pressure applied by the cigarette companies. None of us smoked, so the two youngest, Norma and Bob, were chosen to share one mask. Norma was in nursing school, so she made an impromptu comparison of each of their heart rates, with and without oxygen, at the different altitudes we flew, up to 16,000 feet. She found, of course, that the pulse quickens and the heart pumps harder in the oxygen–starved air at high altitude. The body attempts to adjust for the low oxygen content by increasing its heart rate.

Norma's amazing find was that the slowing of the pulse rate on the person who had been without the mask for a few moments, was very quick, once oxygen was inhaled. Our bodies are indeed very adaptable machines.

After graduating, Norma accepted a posting to a hospital in Long Beach, California. Although I was sorry to see her work so far from home, I knew that my aeroplane and training would permit Vivienne and myself to visit her often. And visit her we did. The problem was that she and Vivienne always wanted to go shopping in their free time. I get bored very quickly with this routine. Fortunately, their favorite shopping center was in Orange County, close to the John Wayne Airport.

I spent many hours at that airport, wandering up and down the rows of private planes parked outside on their tarmac. I saw a lot of different ideas for open air storage of an aeroplane on that airport and have included four pictures. I had never before seen an aeroplane so completely wrapped up against the elements. Under–neath, I am sure the paint must be still just like new. One Twin Comanche owner who had his plane for sale, made certain, with a chain and padlock, that no one would fly it away until it was paid for.

Even the propellor is wrapped as protection against the elements and birds.

Twin Comanche for sale — including padlock key.

Most of the owners had a storage box of some sort inside their allotted space on the tie–down line. I was intrigued by the vast difference between two of these containers. Both planes were away from their storage spots when I took the pictures, so I never met the owners. I couldn't help speculating on how different these

Opposite ends of the Storage Spectrum.

two people must be. I also thought I might prefer to fly in the aeroplane owned by the pilot who used the neat little two storey house to store his tools and extra oil.

By this time, I had finished building in the north and had traded down my six place Piper Aztec for the smaller, four place

Twin Comanche. There were always several like mine parked at Orange County. I remember how I envied the ones with the extra fuel tanks on their wing tips. *I don't think that I really appreciated, at the time though, just how important that extra fuel could be in certain situations.*

5

Progressive Challenges

CIRCLING THE CARIBBEAN

Now that we had successfully flown to most places in North America and The Bahamas, the next logical challenge was to fly to another continent. I was still limited by standard capacity fuel tanks, with a little over four hours range at normal cruising speeds. This made South America the only other continent within range. So South America it was!

Jim arranged for the necessary time off. As we both had scuba certificates, we decided to look for two more similarly qualified adventurers. We found them in our friends Dexter and John and started to plan the trip. We agreed to circle the Caribbean and divide our time on the ground between the sights to be seen both above and below sea level.

A study of recommended locations provided us with three well–spaced scuba rest stops on the circuit and lots of exciting new countries to visit. By the time the route was selected, it was agreed we could carry the four persons but would be limited to one small personal bag each. It would not be possible to guarantee arrivals to hotels along the way, so no firm reservations were made. Consequently, four very light space–age sleeping bags were brought along for emergencies.

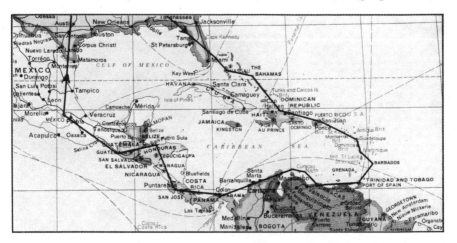

Caribbean Chart

Caribbean flight–planning booklets and charts were obtained from the Canadian and American pilots' associations. I wrote to the addresses provided for each of the en route countries. I advised them of our plans and approximate arrival dates and requested their written permission. Unfortunately, the addresses I was given were really intended for obtaining tourist information and advertising brochures – and that is what we received. We never did get any letters of permission or refusal before departure, but I don't think it did any harm. At least one tower controller in Honduras said he had received word from his superiors to expect us.

It was early March when we set off from our staging stop in Nassua, into the brilliant Bahamian sky, for a one hour fifteen minute flight to the diver's island of San Salvador (formerly Watlin Island). The island was an American Air Force base during World War II, so there is a good asphalt runway located just one quarter mile away from the diving resort hotel called Riding Rock Inn. There, we rented a cottage and had lunch. By 1400 hrs., we were thirty feet under water in one of the finest diving spots in the world. We got close to Squirrel Fish, French Angel Fish, Yellow Grunt, Parrot Fish, Barracuda and dozens of others I didn't know the names of. Several large friendly groupers stayed with us throughout the entire dive. One in particular followed me wherever I went. He seemed intensely curious about me and my odd looking friends. We also swam through schools of Yellow Grunt fish so thick they nearly blocked off all the light from above. We

The author's special underwater friend.

became friends with all the species except the Barracuda. I suspect that this dangerous looking fish has very few friends – even among other fish.

The diving was so good there we decided to rent an underwater Nikonos camera for the next day. We took turns taking underwater pictures – a thirty–six exposure roll on each of two dives. We began the day with a deep ''wall'' dive, while the second one was shallow so that decompression wouldn't be necessary. The school of underwater photography on the island had our films developed by 8 pm the same night, and we were quite pleased with our first efforts.

In the morning, when we attempted to buy some of the aviation gas advertised on the flight charts and in the brochures, we found out that the locals had burned it all up in their automobiles! We were assured there was lots on the diving island of Providencialles, in The Ciacos Islands to the south, so we decided to go there for our refill and a couple more dives. The next morning, we flew another hour and twenty minutes to this island and were advised that they were also out of gas (for the same reason). However, there was still plenty on South Ciacos Island, forty miles away. We decided to check into the hotel, have a dive or two, and go on the next day. We planned to stop at South Ciacos to fill our half empty tanks, and head for Port Au Prince in Haiti.

The winds were too strong for the dive boats, so we did some sightseeing on the island instead. There must be a lot of wind on the island, because a storm four months earlier had washed sand up and blocked the mouth of the harbor, and it hadn't been opened yet. The harbor still contained about twenty pleasure yachts which had originally planned to stop there only a day or two.

In the morning, we talked to an inter-island pilot who informed us they had **just** run out of avgas on South Ciacos and that all these islands were now waiting for a tanker with some more fuel. No one knew when the supply ship would arrive, so it was time to make an alternate plan.

The night before in the bar, several of the locals had recommended a visit to the Dominican Republic instead of Haiti. At the airport, our inter-island pilot told us that Puerto Plata in the Dominican Republic **always** had lots of gas, as very few planes went there. We checked the winds and our remaining fuel and decided we could just reach Puerto Plata with the required 45 minutes reserve. It was our only option, so that is where we went.

When we landed on their brand new 7,000 ft. paved runway and taxied up to the recently constructed Puerto Plata terminal, we

Tire spraying crew and friend at Puerto Plata deciding who will pump and who will spray.

were the only plane in sight. Very soon eight attendants came out to service us. We were now about to experience southern bureaucracy in action. The first three-man team wanted $10.00 to disinfect our tires with their garden sprayer – one collected the money, one pumped up the sprayer and the third sprayed the tires for germs. The gas truck attendants refused all credit cards and traveller's cheques and moved to fill us only after I produced a fistful of American cash, which I had brought along for just such an emergency.

The next man up was the customs inspector, followed by an official who introduced us to a form that you really should not leave home without. It is called the "General Declaration Form" and is available in pads of about 100 copies from all pilots associations for a couple of dollars a pad. If you don't have your own, the price from the customs officials is a couple of dollars a sheet. We found that entry required anywhere from three copies to about twelve, depending on the country.

The airport manager was next. We paid him the landing fee. He taught us the value of carrying lots of small bills, because he had no change! Another interesting thing we learned was that the pilot and co-pilot of any aircraft, no matter how small, normally do not require a passport in the Caribbean, South or Central America. They also don't pay entry or departure taxes. Our passengers, however, required all of the above and a visitor's permit.

Reflecting on our arrival in Puerto Plata, I would strongly recommend that anyone going south of the Bahamas on the east side, or below Mexico on the west side, of the Caribbean take lots of U.S. cash with them. Traveller's cheques aren't readily accepted down there – other than in large hotels. Following this trip, I invested in a money belt and it has been an integral part of my foreign flight kit ever since.

We flew to the east end of the Dominican Republic for the night, to the picturesque little town of Samana. In the morning, we left this wonderful "fuel rich" country and stopped in San Juan, Puerto Rico enroute to our next destination – Guadeloupe. Like a dog never passing a fire hydrant, our recent fuel shortages had taught us never to pass a gas station, especially an American controlled one like San Juan. We refuelled again.

The islands are close together in these waters, and each has its own control area in the surrounding airspace. Even when flying

VFR, it is essential to report entering each new airspace and to prepare estimated times for all the crossing points. Soon after takeoff, we passed St. Croix, St. Kitts and Montserrat. The controller started talking to us in French, then switched to English with a heavy French accent, and we landed at Pointe a Pitre, Guadeloupe. After a no–hassle customs clearance, we hailed one of their Mercedes Benz taxis to take us to Club Caravelle, one of the two Clubs Mediterranean on the island. Jim and John explained to the guardhouse attendants that they were planning on bringing a group to their club during the next year, so we were given a free hand to wander about to see what one gets for approximately $1,000.00 per week, all inclusive.

The facilities were excellent at this Club Med. We started walking along just behind the beach front. As we walked, what began as a family beach gradually changed into a topless beach, then into a topless and bottomless beach. Dexter shot a couple of quick pictures from the hip with his 35 mm camera, but unfortunately, they turned out to contain only pictures of the sand right in front of him. He is currently practicing this photographic technique for his next visit.

That afternoon, we departed for Martinique and found that a fair amount of cloud had developed. We flew under it by dead reckoning, which took us along the east coast of the island of Dominica. This little island was the target of two ill–fated takeover attempts several years ago. A few minutes later, we landed at our destination, La Lamentin airport on Martinique. Once again the controlling and customs were performed in English, and soon we were settled into our hotel in Fort–de–France.

The next morning, Jim and John took a cab to research the local Club Mediterranean, while Dexter and I shopped around town. Prices were high there, and the only shirt I bought in Martinique shrunk about five sizes the first time I washed it.

After lunch, we met up at the airport and took off for our planned rest stop at Barbados. En route, the right engine started to run a little rough. Its engine temperature fell somewhat and so did all the happy chatter about what Jim and John had seen during their visit to their second Club Med. As we looked down at the water below, we drew what comfort we could from the fact that there should still be one good engine to support us if the right one packed up. As a precaution, we donned the inflatable life vests and crossed our fingers and toes. Fortunately, the situation remained stable all the way to Barbados, where we found the trouble to be fouled spark plugs in the right engine – perhaps the result of some bad gas.

In Barbados, our only hassle was with the health inspector. He wouldn't pass us until we bought a can of his favorite disinfectant spray. The airport shops stock about 500 cans, probably at his request, for people like us. Once we showed him our can, he waved us through, never once asking if we had actually used it on the aeroplane!

I was glad I had bought the disinfectant, for it was required at every subsequent stop. Also universally required was that famous General Declaration Form that all officials seem to like so much. *Only the Dominican Republic sprayed our tires instead of the aircraft interior. I am still wondering if they somehow misunderstood the instructions contained on that international form, for everyone else wanted the spray used inside the cabin.*

The following morning, I had the plugs cleaned and test flew the plane. It ran well again, so I returned to the condominium poolside for some R. and R. That evening turned out to be the manager's cocktail party with an outdoor steak dinner and entertainment. Following the dancers and fire-eaters, we entered Dexter in the Limbo contest, and he came away with the prize for second – three drinks for his friends.

We took a cab to the airport the next day. Our cab driver, Lawrence Johnson, turned out to be a delightful gentleman. He told us a story about having asked the priest at his church a question about the stars, which the priest could not answer. Some time later, Lawrence visited his local library. The first book he opened answered his burning question and he became a ''student of the stars'' on the spot. Eventually, he became the island expert on heavenly bodies. He was a most interesting person and his tip was above average because of it.

Once again, it was a beautiful day in the Caribbean. In a little over an hour, we landed at Crown Point Airport in Tobago. We booked a two-hour tour of the island with another interesting cab driver named Hamilton. He drove us through the villages and up to Fort St. George. On the way back, he told us as we passed a local pub, that it was a favorite place on Saturdays for the locals to eat bread and Shark!

The runway at Tobago is too short for jet airliners, so the tourists are brought there by secondary carriers from Trinidad, our next stop. There was lots of fuel in Trinidad, and it was reasonably priced. The supplier though, would not accept payment in more than one currency, and I didn't have enough local money left over from Tobago. The money changers were all closed for a siesta – so once again my roll of US cash came to the rescue. Then we were off for our third and final leg of the day – to Caracas, Venezuela, and our first time on the continent of South America!

The controllers at the oceanfront airport serving Caracas spoke better English than those in Trinidad, but most of the other officials around the airport spoke virtually none. With the help of two Pan Am customer interpreters, we eventually cleared all the local hurdles and checked in for two nights at the nearby Macuto Sheraton.

In the morning, we located an English speaking cab driver who drove us about 30 miles inland to the city of Caracas. He soon became our official source of all we ever needed to know about the area. He bought us a local drink called ''Chee Chaw'', made of rice,

Crowded housing on free hillside land in Caracas.

milk, sugar and ice. We drank it as we ate local dried banana fritters. *He also told us that Caracas thieves often work in pairs on a motorcycle. When they see a lady standing alone on a corner, they ride by, and the rider on the back grabs her purse as they roar off into the crowded streets.*

There are four million people and just under one million cars in this intriguing city of contrasts. Automobile gas is cheap for political reasons, and all the cars seem to be on the road all the time. Men aren't allowed to enter a public park or any government grounds while wearing short pants. The liberator of the whole area from here to Mexico was Simon Bolivar, so everything is named after him, from their airports to their money. Caracas was also the first city I had seen that has a special wide concrete "Parade Concourse" with bleachers on both sides, several blocks long, for the specific purpose of displaying military might.

Although we enjoyed Venezuela, when we checked out with the authorities at the airport, we were understandably unhappy with their landing and parking fees. For a little Twin Comanche parked in the open at the farthest end of the airport, the charges were two dollars per hour, day and night. Our bill to land and park for two nights and one day turned out to be ninety-four U.S. dollars. If we didn't pay - we would not be given clearance for take-off.

We couldn't leave fast enough and took off for the tiny island of Bonaire, sixty miles off the coast. It is one of the Netherland Antilles "ABC" islands of Aruba, Bonaire and Curacao. At their pleasant new airport the charges were just $1.80 for landing and $1.00 per twenty-four hour day for parking - a total of $3.80 for the two nights and two days we were to spend on this friendly little island. *I will always remember that, just sixty miles away, the parking charges were forty-eight times as high!*

We had written ahead to Captain Don, who ran a Bonaire diving resort called Habitat. When we arrived, we found we were expected and the next dive boat was to leave in twenty minutes. We talked them out of their standard preliminary checkout dive, and enjoyed a spectacular dive on their forty-foot reef. At ten o'clock the same night we made another dive - this time right off their dock where it is only 150 ft. to the wall, and where we could have any amount of depth or scenery we wished for a night dive.

The ocean floor at night is covered with black spiny sea urchins, and I was careful not to descend onto their domain. The red and orange colors of the fish and coral really come to life in the under-water lights. Everything was much more brilliant than it had ever been in daylight, filtered through 30 feet or more of blue-green water.

Between dives the next day, we hired a taxi driver named Nick who spoke good English, having spent some time in the U.S. He drove us around the flamingo sanctuary and to the slave huts in the salt gathering areas of the little island. The ocean water is allowed to flood the low lying salt beds, after which the entrance is closed off. The salt water evaporates in the hot sun, and bulldozers scrape up the dried salt for commercial purposes.

Tiny two-man Slave Huts at salt farm on Bonaire.

In the old days, the salt gathering was done by slaves who lived in small, low huts. The slaves originally came from several countries, and to enable them to talk among themselves without their overlords understanding, they pooled their native Por-tuguese, Dutch, English and Spanish languages into a patois all their own called "Papiemento". This hybrid language is still in prominent use on the island. The local fishermen take their catch to the more prosperous and populated island of Curacao. If you want superior scuba diving, however, Bonaire is the island to visit.

In Bonaire, we also visited Trans World Radio which broadcasts with 500,000 watts to the South American continent all night, every night, in several languages. This non-profit operation is sponsored by funds raised in the US and Canada. The transmitter is located there because of the relatively stable government under the Dutch influence, and its proximity to the target South American audience.

On departure day, we went to the airport, cleared customs and took our group airport photo. We usually took this picture on arrival, but in Bonaire you are only permitted to take pictures on the airport when you are leaving – we still don't know the reason for this.

In the air, the right engine started sounding rough again, so I landed at the most westerly of the three Dutch islands, Aruba, for another plug cleaning and a full load of fuel for the long hop to Panama. Our estimated time to Panama was four hours, so we flew on an economy engine setting which gave us five hours duration at 6,500 feet. We arrived in four hours and five minutes, with fifty five minutes fuel reserve, took a taxi tour of the city and checked into our hotel.

Our next destination in Central America was another scuba diving resort, on the island of Roatan, some thirty miles off the North coast of Honduras. Our two choices for an en route fueling stop appeared to be either Managua, Nicaragua, or in San Jose, Costa Rica. I decided on the latter due to the instability of Nicaragua.

Before leaving Panama, we cleared with Air Traffic Control to permit us to make an aerial tour of the Panama Canal on the way out. I was cleared for the East side of the canal and was surprised to learn, on checking the map, that the center line of the canal is more than ninety degrees off the East–West route I had envisaged since early school days. I was also surprised at how little of the canal is man-made and how much of it is natural waterway. The canal's chief architect was Gustav Eiffel, designer of the Eiffel Tower in Paris. The canal is often a bottleneck, and we saw thirty to forty freighters anchored off its North port called Colon, awaiting their turn through.

In just over two hours, we arrived in San Jose, Costa Rica, and immediately it was obvious that we were in a very friendly place – that is, as long as you are not running guns or drugs. Near our parked aeroplane, was a large single engine Cessna and its cargo of illegal guns being guarded by an armed soldier, while its pilot was downtown receiving some swift and rough justice. We were well treated, however, and were fueled in fifteen minutes, which is fast for Latin America. After lunch in the pleasant airport restaurant, we were on our way again.

Three hours in the air at 10,000 feet brought us over LaCeiba, a port-of-entry on the North coast of Honduras. Our instruments told us we were over top the airport, but it had become obscured by cloud. Our charts showed an 8,000 ft. mountain range five miles inland from the waterfront so we went well out over the ocean, made our letdown through some thin holes to 3,000 ft., then back in under the cloud to the airport.

We gave nearly everybody in sight $5.00 to apply their stamp to our immigration and customs papers and took off again under cloudy skies for our final dive stop, thirty miles away, on Roatan. The lone runway on the island is short and made of coarse black rock. All tourist divers are brought in by DC 3 (C47) – except us. When we landed, Jim put the Comanche down "quite firmly," and although we didn't know it until the next day, **the landing caused a hairline crack in the right landing gear oleo casing.**

The winds were so strong that there was no diving this day or the next, so we decided to leave in the morning for the Aztec ruins in Tikal, Northern Guatemala.

When we got to the airport, we saw our collapsed oleo. Since there was no fuel, no mechanic, and very little English spoken outside of the scuba hotels, we made a soft-field takeoff and departed for the mainland. We then discovered that, if the right landing gear is not properly extended, its oleo switch prevents the wheels from coming up. This is because, if the gear did come up in this shortened state, the right wheel wouldn't reach the hole in the underside of the wing, into which it is supposed to go. We flew, with the gear down, back to La Ceiba (where the DC 3's come from) in search of a mechanic.

We found one but couldn't converse with him, until I had a brainwave – get one of the English speaking tower controllers to translate for us. Brilliant! But it didn't work. La Ceiba is an international airport but the least important one in all of Honduras. The controllers there are just learning to control in the International English language. They had learned to repeat only a limited number of necessary phrases like "Cleared to land," "Cleared to take off," etc. They hadn't the foggiest idea of the English world for "cracked oleo."

Since my scheme hadn't worked, I used sign language to give the mechanic a free hand to do whatever he thought best – and he turned out to be the "brilliant" one. He reasoned, that although air leaked out of the oleo through the hairline crack, perhaps thick oil wouldn't. He was right! It was getting dark when he finished work, so we went into town for the night.

On the bus to town was an eighteen year old boy from California, who had been bumped off the last DC 3 for the day to Roatan because there were no more seats. Instead of sleeping in the safety of his uncle's hotel on Roatan island, he was being forced to stay overnight in this strange foreign country, all by himself, on the first night he had ever been away from home. His name was Steve, and he attached himself to our little group, since we were the only English speaking, American looking, people in sight. *At the hotel he was awarded a free private room by the airline, but he wouldn't sleep in it. Steve was going to sleep in the same room with us, even if he had to sleep on the floor at our feet. In the end, I let him sleep in the room with Jim, and I took his single room down the hall.*

In the morning, we all went back to the airport to see how the oleo had held out. The mechanic was also on the bus, coming out on a Saturday, his day off, to see if the four visiting pilots needed any further help. The oleo had dropped only about one sixteenth of an inch out of its four inch extension, so we thanked this clever mechanic and set off for our revised destination – Tapachula in the Southwest corner of Mexico. We cancelled our plan to land in the jungle airport of Tikal, as we felt we should only put the plane down very gently for the remainder of the trip. The oleo case did last all the way home, with a drop of only about one-half inch.

After a thorough narcotics inspection and a quick lunch, we were away VFR to Mexico City. We passed the white topped Mount Popacotapetl, crossed the last ridge into Mexico City and landed in a dust storm which surrounded the airport.

The following morning, we hired a cab for a four hour tour. The tour was interesting but, as usual, so was the cab driver. He had two families – a wife and three children in Mexico City and a wife and four children in Acapulco. He told us it was legal to have two wives in Mexico, as long as both were not in Mexico City. He got two weeks holiday every three months to spend with his wife in Acapulco and said the families did not know of each other. It might have been an "old wives tale," but he showed us photos of each family and all seven children. He was quite casual about it and thought we might carry the recommendation back home with us.

At the end of our city tour, we said good-bye to Jim and John at the airport, because their allotted vacation time was up. The next day, Dexter and I headed for home. We had lots of carrying capacity now that the other two had left. We picked up bags of oranges and grapefruit in Texas. I made stops at Wiley Post Airport at Oklahoma City and Sioux Falls, South Dakota, on the long trek northward.

It was a trip the four of us will remember for a long time. We packed a lot of experience and sightseeing, both above and below mean sea level, into three weeks. We gained a knowledge and understanding of the peoples in the islands and southern countries by meeting them by ourselves. Nearly everyone we met was great. A few had their hands out but, for the most part, they were friendly and cooperative.

Our horizons now extended all the way to South and Central America.

6

Progressive Challenges

TRANSATLANTIC AIR RALLY

The last time I had been to Europe was in 1950. When I finished my year of postgraduate study in London, I bought an English motorcycle and set off for a glorious summer on the continent. That stalwart little machine carried me across France, Italy, Switzerland, Germany, Holland, Denmark and Sweden, nearly 7,000 miles. Now, in 1985, there was an opportunity to visit Europe again - this time in my Twin Comanche.

The aviation magazines were carrying advertisements for the ''First Transatlantic Air Rally For Light Aircraft.'' The route chart they published showed the longest leg between fuelling stops to be 450 nautical miles, from Frobisher Bay, Baffin Island to Gothab, Greenland. Crossing the North Atlantic to the Continent of Europe and competing with a number of other small aircraft in a rally, certainly seemed like an interesting new challenge.

Some years before, when I owned my single engine Cessna 172, I entered the Governor General's Canadian Air Rally. The competition is held annually and is open to all aircraft. The winning captain receives the Governor General's Trophy for a year and a cash prize of $500.00. The navigator in the winning aircraft is given a much prized Hudson's Bay Blanket coat. The year I

The author (L) and G. Johnson (R) with Governor General's Canadian Air Rally Trophy.

entered, there were forty–six aircraft in the competition from the United States and Canada. My navigator, Gordon Johnson, and myself, completed the various assignments, along the prescribed aerial course, with less penalty points than anyone else and won. This made me believe I could also be competitive in a transatlantic air rally.

However, I wondered if I had enough courage to head out over the North Atlantic Ocean, toward Europe, in my little Comanche. The last time I had exhibited such a lack of concern for

Bullfighting in Tenerife, Canary Islands.

my safety, was fourteen years earlier on a holiday to Tenerife, Canary Islands. Vivienne and I were at a night club, appropriately called ''El Toro.'' Following a floor show, champagne and liqueurs, all the guests were invited outside to the night club's own ''Bull Ring'' to watch six of their number learn the rudiments of bull fighting – using Live Bulls!

Buoyed by false courage, I volunteered. I thought I could watch the others and see how it was done before I faced my bull. *Unfortunately, I was selected first!* The six bulls were sent into the ring to do battle in order of their size, however. I was therefore lucky enough to draw the smallest bull used that night. With help from the professional matador, I managed to wave the red cape at my four-legged adversary a number of times and still escape injury as he charged me. Three of the six neophite matadors were thrown by their bulls that evening and one was injured. I presume that is why they had us sign a waiver before we entered the ring! Anyway, if I could muster up enough courage to fight a bull, I should be able to handle the North Atlantic.

The rally schedule called for a nine day trip from the Statue of Liberty in New York, to the Eiffel Tower in Paris. Adding a three day visit in Paris, and four or five days flying home, I calculated an overall trip of just under three weeks. They say that a good pilot

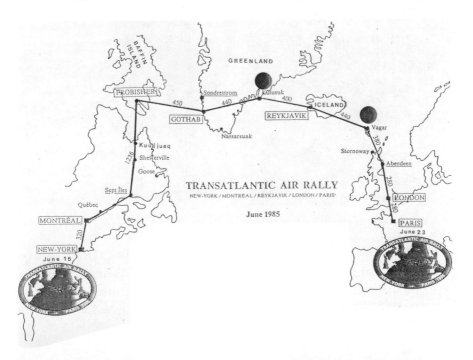

and co-pilot go hand in hand – except, of course, through the terminal building. Neither of my sons could get that much time off from work, but each could manage enough vacation time to travel one way with me. It was decided that Jim would be my companion during the rally on the way to France. Bob and his new bride, Sharon, would travel by commercial airline to Paris and become my crew on the way home. Sharon had recently obtained her private pilot's license, so she was jumping right into the deep end of this cross country flight business with both feet – and hoping they would stay dry, I suspect.

The 4,781 mile rally was intended to test the crews on their accuracy of map reading, correct estimation of fuel burns, flying over specific points at predicted times, precision arrivals at airports, and being able to put the aircraft's wheels down on a white line painted across the runway. A total of $20,000.00 in prizes was offered for the three best scores in the rally.

The Fonger entry — Jim, Don, Sharon, Bob.

They soon had their limit of entries, including about thirty single aircraft and one from the Flying Fongers. When the list of entrants was distributed, it contained forty-six American names, twelve from Europe and nineteen from Canada. Only two cities in the world had more than one entrant - New York City had two and, to my surprise, Winnipeg had four. When I pointed out to my wife the large proportion of local pilots who had entered, her comment consisted of five words: ''There are more Airheads here!''

We had to obtain insurance policies acceptable to the U.S. Government, in case we were forced to land at Sondrestrom, their air force base in Greenland. We also required oxygen for high altitude, survival kits for wilderness areas, and approved life jackets and rafts for over-water flights. We filled Sharon's return trip seat on the way over with a courageous, non-pilot friend of mine and took out the fourth seat to provide space for what we had to carry. We put all the recommended survival equipment on board, even though some sources advised that we would have less than three minutes to get out of the thirty -three degree water and into our life rafts. *Furthermore, if we were over thirty years old - forget it!*

Each aircraft was to have a colorful name for the rally. One pair chose ''The Wrong Brothers.'' Others were called ''Never Give Up, Mickey Mouse, The Looney Mooney and Plane Crazy.'' I named mine ''The Golden Boy'' after the gold- covered figure that sits atop the legislative building in the Province of Manitoba. The ''Golden Boy'' had originated as a gift to the province, from the people of France during the first world war. Our Provincial Premier provided me with a ''Golden Boy'' plaque to carry and deliver to Jacques Chirac, the mayor of Paris. This was to be a goodwill gesture, commemorating the gift of that magnificent statue to Manitoba many years before.

The Mayor of Gimli in Manitoba, gave me a Viking Plaque for the Mayor of Reykjavik in Iceland, because the Canadian town of Gimli is also known as ''Little Iceland.'' Pilots may recognize that Gimli, an old wartime training airport, is also known as the world's most famous glider airport. An airline pilot, flying a Boeing 767 commercial jet airliner, that had been fueled in metric liters instead of gallons, glided his plane and passengers to safety there when his fuel tanks ran dry en route across Canada.

But on with the Rally. On Saturday morning, June 15, 1985, the Morristown, New Jersey, airport was closed for two and a half hours while the sixty-eight entrants present departed at thirty second intervals for Montreal. The fastest planes departed first, so they wouldn't have to pass anyone in the clouds if the weather deteriorated.

Actually, it was a gorgeous day and, by special arrangement with the Federal Aviation Authorities, we were allowed to fly north up the Hudson River through the center of Manhattan at just 1,500 feet. It was a great start! *We passed the imposing Statue of Liberty, having its one hundred year face lift, on our left. The World Trade Centre and Central Park slipped by on our right. Most of us don't expect to ever have an opportunity like that again.*

Our first stop was at St. Hubert Airport, outside of Montreal. En route, the rally competition consisted of navigating a triangular cross-country course at low altitude and flying an assigned ground speed between checkpoints. The maps supplied were marginal, so it was the aircraft with Loran C navigational equipment that came out on top. This sophisticated navaid enables a pilot to key in the latitude and longitude of any point and fly straight to it without map reading. We did not have this equipment, so along with many others like us, we didn't do very well on this exercise.

On arrival at St. Hubert, we were to make three landings as close as possible to a white line painted across the runway. Since

Landing on the white line at St. Hubert, Quebec.

three circuits take ten to fifteen minutes to complete, it didn't take a rocket scientist to figure out that the sixty-five aircraft, which had taken off only thirty seconds apart, were bound to bunch up at the end. Predictably, it was a mess! Some of the more sophisticated turbocharged aircraft couldn't do a touch and go on the short runway assigned to the exercise. They were penalized 240 points for the two landings they couldn't do, even though it was not their fault. Others flew circles outside the airport area for so long, awaiting their turn, that they ran short on fuel and were forced to land on another runway. They suffered 360 penalty points for something over which they had no control.

That night, the first leg standings were posted and we were twenty-fifth out of sixty-eight. We went to the lobster boil held for the rally participants and drowned our sorrows. The party was fun, and an opportunity to meet everyone on the rally.

Everything about the rally, except the competition itself, was great. We were put up in the best available hotels and in school dormitories across the North where hotel rooms are scarce. The food was great, the scenery was great, the fellowship was great. The local people were excited and glad to have us there — it was an experience of a lifetime!

The author with Inuit Children beside the ''Golden Boy'' at Frobisher Bay, on Baffin Island. The children are blowing souvenir aeroplane-shaped whistles given out by the Fongers along the rally course.

From Montreal, the next leg was a long one, 1,236 nautical miles (1,420 statute miles) up to Frobisher Bay (now named Iqualit) on Baffin Island. We had reached another new horizon. For the first time, we were almost at the Arctic Circle. *Most people I have asked have only a vague conception of what the arctic circle really is. It is an imaginary line, which runs parallel to the equator at sixty–six degrees, thirty minutes, north latitude. North of the Arctic Circle there are twenty–four hours of daylight on June 21, and twenty–four hours of darkness on December 21.*

Since we were flying the rally from June 15 to 23, we didn't have to worry about night flying. Clouds were another thing, however, and the departure intervals from Montreal were stretched out to provide separation on instrument conditions. Because of this, many aircraft had no chance of making their arrival at Frobisher anywhere near the time they had predicted the night before. These predictions had been made, based upon a published departure time list that was never adhered to. Somehow we ended up third best for this long leg and moved from twenty–fifth to fifth position.

On our third leg, we flew from Frobisher, north to the Cape Dyer beacon, just above the Arctic circle and then to Godthab, the capital city of Greenland, on its west coast. There, they have carved a rock shelf into a runway. It resembles an aircraft carrier in dry dock but it is level, paved, and has a good instrument approach. We maintained our 5th position with an average performance on this leg, but several pilots tried so hard to improve their rally standing that they damaged their aircraft.

A Twin Beechcraft pilot was late as he approached over the water, so he powered his plane onto the runway in an attempt to pick up time. Apparently, he believed in the old adage which says, ''It is better to be dead than look bad!'' He bounced when he hit, came down on one wheel and bent one of his propellors. Fortunately, no one was injured, and he had another propellor flown in from New York two days later. He may have saved ten penalty points, but it cost him about ten thousand dollars.

A single–engine Mooney pilot found himself early on the same approach and held his plane off the runway to use up time. He must have believed the old adage, ''There is no approach so bad that it can't be saved.'' He didn't put his wheels down until there was less than one half of the 3,000 foot runway remaining. He slammed on his brakes and held them tight until he blew a tire, wrecked a wheel, and ran off the side of the runway. He too saved some very expensive penalty points. I couldn't help thinking of the saying "The only difference between men and small boys is the cost of their toys."

A picturesque Greenland Fiord just prior to crossing the Ice Cap beyond.

From Godthab, the next stop was Reykjavik, Iceland, 840 nautical miles away. The first half of the route was across the Greenland ice cap – probably the bleakest 400 miles on earth. The second half was only slightly better – across iceberg infested waters! There is a small airport at Kulusuk on the East coast of Greenland, but, when we were due to depart, it was closed because of weather. We didn't have enough fuel to challenge the vicious head winds, that had come up over the ice cap, and go straight to Iceland without making an intermediate landing. The ice cap is over 300 miles long and about 7,000 feet thick and is reported to have swallowed up over thirty small planes like mine over the years. The only sensible thing to do was to wait.

During our day of waiting in Godthab, (also called NUUK), we watched several contestants head off over that expanse of deadly ice, only to return when the humbling thought of running out of fuel in that hostile environment caused them to change their mind. An ex–airline pilot flying a single engine Bonanza, had his engine quit over the ice cap. He declared an emergency, but managed to get it started again just before he hit the ice. He returned to Godthab with a rough engine. The mechanics declared the cause to be arcing in his magnetos and wiring due to the cold, high altitude. After repairs, the pilot tested the aircraft but was never able to bring himself to trust it again. As far as I know, that aeroplane went no farther.

There were two other Twin Comanches on the rally. One of them was captained by Dr. Talibi, a cardiologist from Edmonton, Alberta. There is a natural affinity between Twin Comanche pilots, and we spent most of our idle day in Godthab together. I think it was during lunch when we began talking loosely about getting together again in some future year and flying farther than just to Paris. Talk is cheap, of course, and gradually the conversation got around to flying right through Europe and the Third World to Australia. We could sell the aeroplanes there and take a Commercial Jet back home to avoid having to retrace our steps. Jim, being the youngest and keenest of the three, kept insisting that, if we could somehow carry enough fuel to get across the Pacific from Australia, we could have a'' REAL'' adventure and'' Go Right Around The World.'' Dr. Talibi said that, if we ever put such a trip together, he would consider coming with us.

The weather cleared a little, and we snapped back to reality. *Jim and I flew high over the icecap, our knuckles as white as the inhospitable landscape below. Perhaps the name of the radar tracking station halfway along the route said it all. It was officially called ''Sob Story.''* We circled down through 5,000 ft. of cloud into Kulusuk for gas and headed on to Iceland, with another ten or twelve short–range aircraft like ourselves, behind us. When we reached Reykjavik at 8:45 that night, the air rally scoring personnel had all packed up and gone to the banquet. Some pilots in front, and all behind me, (who had waited their turn and had come when they were authorized) were assessed the maximum 360 penalty points for the leg. This unfair penalty effectively ruled many of us out of a decent place in the standings. Jim and I dropped back to 8th position and decided that it just wasn't worth competing for prizes under these conditions. From now on, we would simply enjoy the trip and the comradery, and forget about the competition.

Saturday morning, June 22, we were scheduled to fly from Reykjavik to Aberdeen, Scotland, a distance of 820 miles. Our morning weather briefer advised us that there were strong head winds, severe turbulence below 7,000 feet, and icing in the clouds from the turbulence level to about 13,000 feet. He also advised that Vagar, our fuel stop in the Faroe Islands, was below weather minimums, and the airports at both Vagar and Stornoway in Scotland were closing for the weekend at 1,700 hrs. This was no way to start the day!

Following the briefing, Jim and I sat in the weather office with all the other long-faced pilots, wondering how in the world we were going to get to the windup banquet in Paris on Sunday night.

The long-range planes headed off to Aberdeen, and the rest of us listened intently to the weatherman's new idea for those of us who could fly only 800 miles in still air before taking a bath in ice water. His idea was to go around the island, below the thick cloud, to a small Icelandic airport called "Hofn," gas up, and then go to Stornoway for fuel before proceeding to Aberdeen. This route would save some 250 miles over the route from Reykjavik to Aberdeen direct. The catch was that the weather at Stornoway was marginal, and if it got much worse while we were en route, there was no alternative except the ocean again. So, working on the theory that anyone who would go for that idea could be sold the Brooklyn bridge, Jim and I didn't buy it. Several pilots did try to circle Iceland, but they were nearly all back in an hour or so saying that they had just encountered the worst turbulence of their lives at that low altitude.

In the meantime, Jim was watching the hourly weather reports on Vagar, and at noon he advised me of a slight improvement there – not enough to land yet, but an improvement. I suggested that if it improved again at 1,300 hrs., we would take off and have a look for ourselves. By flying high, and using oxygen, we could have radio contact all the way and receive any updated weather reports on our destination. *If the clouds didn't continue to lift at Vagar after we took off, we would return to Iceland and put Jim on a jet back to Baltimore where he had to be at work Monday morning for sure. We couldn't wait any longer before taking off, because it was a three hour flight to Vagar and the airport there was to close at 1700 hrs.*

At 1,300 hrs., the Vagar weather did look a little better so we flight–planned and took off. When four or five others found out what we were up to, they bought the idea and took off behind us.

The weather kept improving, and our small group cleared Vagar by 1,700 hrs. as they were closing for the week end. We all departed with full tanks for Aberdeen, where their ceilings were right at the minimums for that airport, about 200 feet. This time, however, there was an alternate if required. South of Aberdeen the weather was much better and there are a lot of airports in England.

The Golden Boy crew over England, knowing they had successfully crossed the North Atlantic.

One after another, our group landed safely in Aberdeen. The instrument approaches and lighting there are first class – probably due to their continuous foggy weather.

After a night's sleep, we were back at the airport Sunday morning and said good–bye to our passenger, Harold Davies, who was leaving us here as planned. Jim and I then made our final rally flight to Paris. The fog was so thick on the Aberdeen airport, that they used a seeing eye half–ton truck with flashing lights to guide us to the button of the active runway. We took off, more by aiming the aircraft than flying it, and broke out of the cloud at about 4000 feet into the bright sunshine. We didn't see much of England or France, except the coasts on both sides of the English Channel, because we were on top of the clouds on instruments all morning.

Just outside of Paris, we descended through the clouds at Pointoise Airport and landed for customs clearance and another landing contest, which by this time we were totally ignoring. After clearing customs, we took off and flew below the cloud, around the outskirts of Paris, to Le Bourget Airport, our final stop. Le Bourget was chosen by the rally organizers, because Lindberg also landed there on his first transatlantic flight in 1927.

We landed just before 1,400 hrs., Sunday, and after a reception at the airport, went to our hotel. Jim quickly changed his clothes and dashed back into the waiting cab for a ride to Charles de Gaulle Airport for his flight back to Baltimore. His total time in Paris after all that flying — was only three hours!

That night at the Alcazar nightclub, amid all the hoopla of a girlie show, the prizes were given out. During one of the breaks in the show, the Canadian Ambassador to France and I participated on stage in a ceremony of handing over the Golden Boy plaque to the deputy for Mayor Chirac of Paris. My official chores and the rally, were over.

The Author presenting the Golden Boy plaque at windup banquet in Paris. Left to right: Gilles Duguay — Canadian First Minister of France. The Author with: Alain Rivron — Paris Councillor on behalf of Mayor Chirac.

TRANSATLANTIC AIR RALLY
BREITLING CUP
NEW-YORK PARIS 1985

FIRST TRANSATLANTIC AIR RALLY
FOR LIGHT AIRCRAFT

ON JUNE 23, 1985

PILOT D. Forger

HAS ARRIVED AT LE BOURGET AIRPORT NEAR
PARIS.
SAME AIRPORT THEY HAVE USED AT THE
TIME OF THE FIRST TRANSATLANTIC FLIGHT
BY CHARLES LINDBERGH IN 1927.
USING A STANDARD LIGHT AIRCRAFT THIS
EXCEPTIONAL RALLY NEW YORK — PARIS
COULD ONLY HAVE BEEN ACCOMPLISHED BY
OUTSTANDING PILOTS.
BREITLING WATCHES AND VAP, ORGANISERS
OF THE RALLY CERTIFY THIS ACHIEVEMENT.

PARIS, 23 JUNE 1985

BREITLING WATCHES
PRESIDENT

BREITLING
1985
TRANSATLANTIC AIR RALLY

The next morning, I went to the airport to check on my fuel and oil and counted the planes that had completed the rally. Others eventually got to Paris over the next few days, but on Monday morning there were only 39 aircraft at Le Bourget out of the original 68 starters. At least 30 of those on the tarmac were long range planes which did not have those two difficult fuel stops, Vagar and Kulusuk. Most of those not present were still in Iceland waiting for better weather and for airports to reopen.

The final rally posting placed us in 12th position overall – not bad considering that we didn't even pick up our contest envelopes for the last two legs.

In Paris I met my other son, Bob, and his wife, Sharon. They had flown over in a commercial airliner from Canada to be my co-pilot and crew on the way home.

The trip home also had its exciting moments – especially getting into and out of troublesome Kulusuk in Greenland again. We stopped for sightseeing in Paris, London (where we landed at Biggin Hill), Bournemouth, Reykjavik, Frobisher and Churchill. After Reykjavik, we teamed up again with Dr. Talibi as far as Churchill. Once again, as we overnighted in the Churchill hotel, we talked about that far fetched horizon – a flight around the world. We decided that, if we ever did try such a thing, it would probably be a lot safer to have two identical Twin Comanches flying together, than to try it alone. *I don't think that either of us, at that moment, actually though we would ever do it.*

In the morning, we departed Churchill for our respective homes. Fortunately, my aeroplane had performed flawlessly throughout the entire trip. When I got home, I took a bottle of the very best to each of the two mechanics who had serviced the aeroplane prior to the rally.

Upon returning, we were advised of three more rally mishaps. A Mooney pilot had his engine quit at 16,000 feet over the Greenland icecap but got it started again at 8,000 feet as he prepared to ditch in the water near Kulusuk. He was lucky.

The eldest crew in the rally, a pair of gentlemen from Maryland, one seventy-seven and the other eighty-two, ran out of gas three miles from the runway at Frobisher Bay. They managed to put their plane down on a part of the only six miles of road in the area. They damaged a wing on a road sign but otherwise, came out unscathed. These lucky old–timers proved another rule of flying which says: ''Any attempt to stretch fuel will coincide with an increase in head wind.''

But remember, the name of the rally was ''From the Statue of Liberty to the Eiffel Tower.'' We had flown over the lady in New York on our departure, but because of weather, were not allowed to go near the Eiffel Tower in Paris on our arrival . So, the following day, before we left for home, I packed my flight suit in my bag, and Bob and I went to the tower to take pictures.

At the top of the Eiffel Tower, I took my flight suit out and proceeded to put it on for the final picture. Bob noticed a group of tourists curiously watching me as I climbed into my multi–badged garment. When a small crowd of inquisitive onlookers gathered around me, Bob walked up to me as if I were a total stranger and asked in a loud voice: *''Excuse me Sir! Do you do this jump at the same time every day?''*

7

The Ultimate Challenge

PLANNING – THE ROUTE

It took awhile for the excitement of that Transatlantic Air Rally to wear off. After several months however, the possibility of making a flight around the world kept creeping into my thoughts more and more often. Eventually, the idea of Jim and I using the sky to visit "Those Far Away Places With Strange Sounding Names" became a fixation, and the only solution was to start the planning process and DO IT!

The first problem was to figure out where to start. Obviously, there were considerations to be made with both the aircraft and the trip itself. Logically, the foremost considerations were who was going and what route we would take.

Since Jim had initiated the idea, he would be my co-pilot. He was to finish his Cardiac Surgery residency at Johns Hopkins Hospital in Baltimore at the end of June, 1987. He also had to start his practice on the staff of a Harvard hospital in Boston in early September of the same year. That made it obvious – he and I would make the trip during the 60 days of July and August. Anyone else who wanted to join our adventure would have to be able to get away in that same time frame.

Dr. Tal Talibi, our friend from the air rally, quickly announced that he was still anxious to make the flight. His aircraft was a near duplicate of my turbocharged Twin Comanche. Since identical aeroplanes would fly well together, this was encouraging. The bad news was that he didn't know of a qualified co-pilot who could make the trip with him. Jim did. He had a young friend from Washington, D.C., Ken Bamford, who had a private license, with several hundred flying hours. Ken was also willing to upgrade his training, to include an instrument rating on twin engine aircraft, before the proposed departure date – a year and a half away.

For awhile we had a third captain, flying a larger and more sophisticated Beechcraft Duke. During the planning stages, however, he encountered medical problems, and we were back to two aeroplanes and four people. This turned out to be the ideal number. The two identical aircraft could each carry different spare parts which could service either aircraft. By flying in formation over the oceans, if one crew was forced to ditch, the other crew could stay with them long enough to report their situation and location to the rescue center. We also found out later that four people was often the absolute maximum for compact third world taxis and tour cars.

So the Flight Around The World was to be flown with two crews – my son Jim and myself in my Twin Comanche, and Tal and Ken in the other.

Like a river rushing to the sea, we knew now that we couldn't stop. We all met at my house, laid out a world map and started

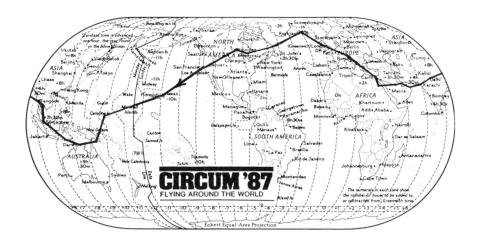

drawing lines around it. *It soon became obvious that there were many considerations to be taken into account in deciding on a route. What countries will allow us to land? Where are their airports of entry, with customs and immigration available? At what hours? Is there 100 octane aircraft fuel available or just Jet fuel? How far can we fly without refueling? Will they bring in drums of fuel for us if they have enough notice? Do they require prior permission to land or overfly, and what information do they require before they will give this permission?*

Fortunately, Ken had brought to the meeting a copy of the International Flight Information Manual, available from the U.S. Department of Transportation in his home town of Washington, D.C. It contained the necessary information on all member countries of the International Civil Aviation Organization (ICAO). Many of the countries required several pages in this manual to list their requirements and information. I have included as an example, one of the simpler countries, Oman, to illustrate what is generally required for a private flight into a foreign country, outside of continental North America. (See Overleaf)

It was mutually agreed that we would not attempt to break any records. Our purpose was to combine education and sightseeing with a flying adventure. For every day we flew, we planned to take the next day off and find out as much as we could about the country into which we had just flown. With this in mind, the four of us wrote down all the places we wanted to visit and all the things we wished to see around the world. To fulfill all the wish lists would have taken at least twice the time available, so a lot of compromising was necessary. The final plan included about thirty flight days and thirty sightseeing days. Instead of touring all of Australia, we could only afford time for a single stop at Darwin. Everyone wanted to visit Bali, the Land of the Gods. *We also agreed to visit as many third world countries as possible, because these were places to which we would not likely return at a future date.*

From the information manual, we determined that there was no Avgas 100 available in Rangoon, Burma, or in Kathmandu, Nepal. Fortunately, upon request, fuel in barrels could be obtained in Dacca, Bangladesh, between Burma and Nepal. A distance check confirmed that our aircraft could survive on the one good drink available in this area, and our routing started to take shape. Jim and I wanted very much to scuba dive in Truk, Micronesia, for

OMAN

PERSONAL ENTRY REQUIREMENTS

PASSPORT: Required.
VISA: Required.
HEALTH & IMMUNIZATION: *Yellow Fever Vaccination Certificates are required for all travellers arriving from infected areas. The U.S. Public Health Service reports that a malaria risk exists throughout the country.*
OTHER: None.

EMBASSY INFORMATION

OMAN'S EMBASSY IN THE UNITED STATES

ADDRESS: Embassy of the Sultanate of Oman, 2342 Massachusetts Ave., N.W., Washington, D.C. 20008.
TELEPHONE: *(202) 387-1980 through 1982*

UNITED STATES' EMBASSY IN OMAN

ADDRESS: *P.O. Box 966, Muscat, Oman*
TELEPHONE: *738-231 through 233, and 738-006.*
TELEX: *3785 AMEMBUS ON*
PUBLIC HOURS: *Saturday through Wednesday, 7:30 AM to 5:00 PM.*

AIRCRAFT ENTRY REQUIREMENTS

All private and non-scheduled commercial aircraft overflying or landing for commercial or non-commercial purposes must obtain prior permission from the Director General of Civil Aviation, P.O. Box 204, Muscat, Sultanate of Oman (TELEGRAPHIC ADDRESS: CIVAIR MUSCAT/ TELEX: 5418 DGCAOMAN ON) at least 72 hours prior to arrival. All requests must include: (a) name of aircraft operator; (b) aircraft type and registration marks; (c) dates and times of arrival and departure; (d) place of embarkation and disembarkation abroad of passengers and cargo; (e) purpose of flight; (f) number of passengers and type and amount of cargo; (g) name, address and business of charterer, if any; and (h) names of crew members.

CORPORATE AIRCRAFT CONSTRAINTS

Cabotage not permitted for residents or nonresidents. In special cases, may be permitted by Directorate General of Civil Aviation, subject to clearance by the military. Corporate aircraft subject to same civil aviation regulations as commercial flights. Flights to/from Israel or PDRY explicitly prohibited; flights to/from Ethiopia or Angola routinely denied.

SPECIAL NOTICES

1. Aircraft destined to or departing from an Israeli Airport shall not be permitted to overfly or land.
2. Violations to Omani airspace and restricted areas will expose the aircraft concerned to the dangers of firing without prior notice.

INTERNATIONAL NOTAM OFFICE

MUSCAT OOMSYN

AERODROMES OF ENTRY

DOD Enroute Supplement/Chart: EUROPE, N. AFRICA and MIDEAST L20,H14

Muscat/Seeb		OOMS	CIVAIR MUSCAT		5418 DGCAOMAN ON
23°36'N, 58°17'E	H118	L6,7,9	100LL,JA1	*Customs—24. WGT-CAT—B-747.*	
Salalah		OOSA	CIVAIR SALALAH		7655 DGCAOMAN ON
17°02'N, 54°06'E	H89	L6,7,9	100LL,JA1		

reasons I will describe later in the book, so this was included as a stop. Tal wished to visit his birthplace in Istanbul, Turkey and also Geneva, Switzerland, where he took his medical degree. Ken had relatives in Honolulu and wanted to see Iceland. Singapore was the best stop for routine servicing of the aircraft, which obviously had to be given due consideration in the planning process.

Once the route was established, the next decision was whether to go East or West. Our investigation determined that, although most of the prevailing upper winds favor a flight heading East, there were arguments for going Westward as well. I felt that we should fly the two long Pacific ocean legs, of approximately fifteen hours each, while the aeroplanes and pilots were fresh and anxious for the challenge. The amount of fuel required for these two legs dictated additional fuel tanks in the cabin and uncomfortable conditions for the pilots. By going West, we could take one tank out and move the second one back in the cabin as soon as we reached the Marshall Islands. This would greatly increase our comfort for the remainder of the flights. Another important factor was the twenty-four hours of daylight we would pick up as we chased the sunsets around the globe. Instead of losing two hours of daylight flying from Hawaii to Oakland, we could gain two hours by flying the other way. This was a difference of four hours of daylight on this one flight alone. I felt that night flying in unfamiliar surroundings was never a good idea, if it wasn't absolutely necessary. Also, though the upper jet stream normally flows Easterly from Honolulu to California, the trade winds, down closer to the water usually blow the other way. So we went West.

In Washington, D.C., Ken obtained copies of historical wind charts between Oakland and Honolulu for the past several years. It appeared we could anticipate a headwind about one third of the time. We would likely have a neutral wind one third of the time, and for about ten days each month we could reasonably expect a small boost on our tail. We decided we could wait it out in Oakland for the right weather and wind.

I also obtained from the Oakland weather service, a sample of their daily forecast winds en route over the Pacific Ocean to Hawaii. The weather service divides the 2,100 nautical miles into seven 300 mile legs and forecasts the winds separately within each leg. They calculate the effect of each of these winds on an aircraft

```
FHPN KSFO 121840
FOR ROUTE SFO/HNL VIA 31.3N/140W VALID AT 13/1200Z.
                    FLIGHT LEVELS
ZONE   FL050    FL100      FL180      FL240
25  9905 P17  9905 P12  9905 M06  3608 M19  8 ST 005/050
26  9905 P16  9905 P11  1011 M05  0812 M17  DO
27  0410 P14  0711 P10  1117 M06  1121 M17  DO
28  0615 P13  0615 P08  1014 M07  1019 M19 DO
29  0715 P12  0716 P08  0612 M07  0613 M18  1/4 CU 025/080
30  0716 P13  0713 P08  0710 M07  0905 M19  DO
31  0713 P14  0808 P07  9905 M07  2109 M18  DO
32  0712 P15  0708 P09  9905 M06  2616 M17  DO
OVERALL COMPONENTS
    P09       P08        P06        P04
```

```
FHPN KSFO 121840
FOR ROUTE SFO/HNL VIA 31.3N/140W VALID AT 13/1200Z.
                    FLIGHT LEVELS
ZONE   FL050    FL100      FL180      FL240
25  9905 P17  9905 P12  9905 M06  3608 M19  8 ST 005/050
26  9905 P16  9905 P11  1011 M05  0812 M17  DO
27  0410 P14  0711 P10  1117 M06  1121 M17  DO
28  0615 P13  0615 P08  1014 M07  1019 M19 DO
29  0715 P12  0716 P08  0612 M07  0613 M18  1/4 CU 025/080
30  0716 P13  0713 P08  0710 M07  0905 M19  DO
31  0713 P14  0808 P07  9905 M07  2109 M18  DO
32  0712 P15  0708 P09  9905 M06  2616 M17  DO
OVERALL COMPONENTS
    P09       P08        P06        P04
```

Actual forecast winds for 5000 ft. altitude over Pacific Ocean from San Francisco to Honolulu, showing overall tailwind component of 9 knots (10 MPH) forecast for our flight date, July 13, 1987.

Note: The P17, P16, P14 etc. are plus temperatures forecast for each leg in Celsius and are not wind components.

flying the route and publish a net forecasted plus or minus wind factor for the following day. The illustration included is for the seven legs or zones, numbered 25 through 32 for the actual day of our flight. It showed an Overall (Wind) Component from San Francisco (or Oakland) to Honolulu, at an altitude of 5,000 feet (FL050), of Plus 09 knots. This meant they forecast a tailwind of nine knots (about ten miles per hour). That optimistic outlook gave us the extra ounce of courage we needed to commit ourselves to this very long overwater flight. Fortunately, it turned out to be quite accurate.

With our sightseeing destinations established, Ken and Jim obtained from the National Geographic Magazine, a listing of all the issues over the past few years that contained articles about the countries we planned to visit. I borrowed these back issues from a neighbor and, with the aid of a photocopier, prepared a sequence of envelopes, each containing information on one of our proposed stops. We planned to read the information in the applicable envelope the night before we left for, or during the flight to, the next stop on our itinerary. This worked well and helped us decide ahead of time what we most wanted to see during each of our one and a half day whirlwind visits. The articles also contained valuable information on the culture and customs of the people of each country, such as which hand to shake and where NOT to have liquor. **For example, if we were caught with any liquor in Saudi Arabia, our trip would have taken ten years instead of the planned two months.**

There were two possible sources for aviation charts and approach plates. The first was from Jeppeson, the commercial supplier of charts, while the other was the Department of Defence charts from the Defense Mapping Agency in St. Louis Missouri. We chose the latter because it was much cheaper, less bulky and lighter!

A photographic record of the trip was to be made on four 35mm cameras, all using slide film for uniformity and exchangeability. We recognized that none of the four pilot–photographers would take the best picture in all situations. I also knew that the only picture of my aeroplane in flight would be taken from Tal's plane and vice versa. Initially, consideration was given to taking a video camera also, but this idea was dropped to keep weight and confusion to a minimum. It was a fortunate decision, for there were several third world countries where still cameras are permitted but videos are impounded at the airport and returned on departure. Some guides claimed this was to prevent bombs from being smuggled into sites containing national treasures, while others felt it was to encourage potential tourists to visit in person.

Medically, I knew I would be in good hands, since we had a doctor in each crew. Jim was placed in charge of identifying and bringing the necessary medication to soften the effects of any bugs we might pick up in the many different foods we were going to encounter. He also brought along malaria pills for us to begin taking as soon as we left Oakland. Each of us had our vaccinations brought up to date during the months before the flight and obtained current passports.

Since the other three crew members were all fully employed and I was partially retired, I volunteered to obtain all the necessary permissions for the flight. There were two kinds of permission required. We needed authority for the aircraft to land in or overfly eleven of the countries on our route. We also required a number of personal travel Visas.

Approximately five months ahead of our departure date, I wrote the eleven countries which required prior written permission and, in some cases, issued a permit number. I prepared a "worst scenario" fact sheet about the flight, answering every question any of them asked in the Flight Information Manual, and included a copy with each application. Some of them required a stamped envelope to be included for a reply. At first I had no idea how to include a stamp for Burma, Bangladesh, etc. but found that the local post office sells vouchers, which can be exchanged anywhere in the world for a stamp good in the country where the voucher is eventually presented. I had been told that India would likely be the last country to answer – but they were the first. Two months after the first mailing, I had to follow up with Telex and telegrams to those who had not yet responded. Two months after that I repeated the process, and two days before departure, I had obtained permission from all but one country – Saudi Arabia. I dispatched an urgent telegram to them advising that, without their permission, I would have to fly a much more dangerous route through Iraq and Iran. *The idea of them possibly being responsible for our capture or demise brought back an approval the following morning and our aircraft authorizations were complete – or so I thought.*

My research determined that the visas had to be obtained in a number of different cities around the continent. For Canadians, some were issued only in Ottawa, some in Toronto and some in Vancouver. For all of us the only source for a couple of them was in Washington, D.C. The problem was further complicated by the fact that some took two weeks to get, and at least one was only valid for 30 days after it was issued. In all cases, a valid passport had to be presented with the application. One travel agent in Ottawa specialized in going from embassy to embassy in person obtaining visas while he waited. I sent him our four passports and used his services wherever possible. There was not enough time to use the mails so the overnight couriers came to the rescue. As the days dwindled down to a precious few, the last of the visas was finally obtained and our personal paperwork was also complete – or so I thought.

The local newspaper published an article telling of the father and son team attempting to fly around the world together. They also hired me to telephone them periodically during the trip to give them an updated story of our progress. They weren't willing to sponsor the flight, but they were willing to pay me for my articles. So I suddenly became a potential cub reporter as well as amateur world flier.

I also contacted a number of suppliers in the aircraft and fuel industries with regard to possible sponsorship of the flight. Most of them replied with regrets. A few of them offered me the use of their product in return for a report on its performance around the world.

The Champion Spark Plug Company gave me a set of new fine-wire spark plugs. The Armstrong Tire people donated three new eight ply aircraft tires. The Appco Company in Grand Rapids, Michigan, contributed a pair of "Adjust-A-Seat" covers, which have an inflatable bladder in the back that can be adjusted for different positions. The II Morrow Company of Salem, Oregon, gave me the use of an Apollo 604FB Loran C navigation receiver so I could record its performance in all the areas of the world where the Loran C signal exists. All of this equipment performed flawlessly under the stresses of our extended flight.

Add to the above dozens of letters and phone calls between the participants, and one gets an indication of why it takes a year and a half to plan such a flight! **But what about ensuring a Safe Flight? The aeroplanes had to be prepared as well...**

8

The Ultimate Challenge

PLANNING – THE AIRCRAFT

Our plan was to make this flight around the world in the same little aircraft that had served us so well on our Air Rally flight to Paris two years before. My 1970 Twin Comanche was well equipped for flight on this continent, and flights of 400 to 500 miles maximum between fuel stops. The distance from Oakland to Honolulu is 2100 nautical miles, and from Honolulu to Majuro in the Marshall Islands is over 2000. There are no navigational aids on the first leg and only one on the second. Obviously, some careful planning had to take place if these two flights were to be undertaken safely and successfully. *I could see seven major areas of concern.*

Aircraft Dependability

The engines on my aeroplane were at roughly half time between mandatory overhaul. The oil burn had been increasing steadily for the past several hundred hours and was now at about 3 1/2 hours per quart of oil. A 15 hour flight would likely burn between four and five quarts out of a total capacity of eight quarts. I contacted the engine manufacturer, who advised that the engines could run safely on four quarts of oil, but should not be operated on less than that. *The thought of a seized engine somewhere over the Pacific*

Ocean was frightening, so I had all eight cylinders overhauled at the most reputable local engine rebuilding facility. I thought that should definitely bring the oil burn well within limits.

The new spark plugs and tires were installed, and the aeroplane was given a thorough Certificate of Airworthiness inspection and declared fit for the flight. I took pictures of the airframe structural components while the floor was removed for inspection. The purpose of these pictures was to enable me to record the location of the major support members. I could then ensure that they were considered, when the extra fuel tanks we required were installed behind the front seats. I felt the aeroplane was ready.

Authority For The Flight

It was inevitable that I would have to exceed the gross takeoff weight normally certified for the aeroplane, in order to carry sufficient gas to cross the Pacific. I first contacted the Canadian authorities. They were unable to help me since all small aeroplanes crossing the Pacific leave from somewhere in California. The Canadian experience is limited to aircraft crossing the North Atlantic, as most aircraft travelling this route make their North American exit from somewhere in Canada.

I contacted the Southern Cross Ferry Company in California for information and they steered me to the Federal Aviation Authority in Oakland. The Oakland FAA office advised that they had developed special authorization procedures for foreign aircraft wishing to cross the Pacific. They further suggested that, if I used one of the reputable extra-fuel tankers in the area, the procedure and paperwork would be quick and painless. This turned out to be true.

Adequate Fuel for The Pacific

The first thing I did was to install two permanent tip tanks on the ends of the aeroplane's wings. This was an approved and common modification. It provides for roughly two more hours in the air and is a very desirable permanent addition to the plane. I certainly wished many times, during the air rally to Paris, that I had that extra fuel. I located a set of used tip tanks from an unserviceable Twin Comanche and had them installed.

When I inquired from the Southern Cross people how much fuel they carried on their ferry flights to Australia, they advised that they had always used two additional tanks in a Twin Comanche, even when it had tip tanks. The additional tanks were installed in the cabin, one behind the lone pilot and the other pulled up halfway onto the empty co-pilot's seat beside him. They explained that it was necessary to pull this second tank forward to keep the center of gravity within the manufacturer's specified limits. If the center of gravity got behind the recommended aft limit, the aircraft would be unstable in the air and uncontrollable in a stall.

One solution for our trip was to copy their formula and either Jim or myself take a commercial airline for the first two long overwater legs. After that, the weight and balance, with reduced fuel, would permit two pilots on board. This, of course, was

Plywood mockup of first approach at getting extra fuel tanks forward within centre of gravity limits.

unthinkable. My first approach toward the resolution of this problem was to remove the front seats and have two gas tanks made in the shape of seats. Then I planned to install the two seat tanks and put a foam cushion on each one to sit on. My California tanker wisely vetoed this approach as being too complicated. His vast experience with hundreds of ferry tank installations had taught him that complicated fuel transfer procedures between tanks over the ocean, was a very dangerous business.

The eventual solution was to pull BOTH tanks half as far forward as the ferry company had pulled ONE of their tanks. This would achieve the same result from a weight and balance stand-point. The only problem was going to be the discomfort of both

The tiny Twin Comanche cockpit with seats pushed forward by extra fuel tanks. Note life raft between knees of co-pilot and Satnav replacing pilot's arm rest.

pilot and co-pilot. *The best way to appreciate what it was like, is to imagine the pilot in the front bucket seat of a small sports car. Now pull the seat forward on its rails until his knees just touch the dashboard. Lock the seat at that point and bring the seat back perfectly straight up. Pull the aluminum ferry tanks forward tight against the erect seat backs, and fasten both tanks down securely so nothing can move. Those are the conditions we were faced with for those two 15 hour flights over the ocean.* A larger aeroplane would have permitted us more space and security, but Twin Comanches were what Tal and I already owned, and we had to make do with them or stay home. The cockpit photograph should give an idea of our cramped quarters. Our two-man life raft was stored under the co-pilot's knees.

Professional ferry pilots arrive in Oakland, look over the exterior of their assigned aircraft, check the oil and the ferry tank tie down straps, kick the tires and take off for Hawaii. If the aircraft is one with which they are unfamiliar, they read the manual while they fly. I was not that intrepid! I knew that the Twin Comanche's performance would be marginal with two pilots and ferry fuel. I further felt that I needed to know exactly how it would fly, what speeds it would make, and what fuel it would actually burn at the power settings recommended by the manufacturer for long range flight at normal gross weight. So, I flew down to Oakland two months ahead of departure and had the ferry tanks installed, but not connected into the fuel system.

The young aeronautical engineering friend of mine, Ron Renz, had previously helped me test fly the plane at loads, varying from light to the recommended maximum. He was practicing his profession In Kansas, so I stopped there on the way home from Oakland with the ferry tanks in place to do some load testing. I made a number of flights with water in the cabin ferry tanks, adding more water between each flight and recording the aircraft's performance with each incremental load. Jim was still in Baltimore, so we used a series of bags, each filled with twenty–five pounds of lead shot, placed on the other seat and floor. This simulated his weight and the miscellaneous load of radios, maps etc that would be in the plane when we eventually headed over the water. Ron plotted the results and extrapolated the probable aircraft performance to include loads well beyond what would actually be necessary for the two long flights. The data indicated that we were close to the limits – but it would work. I can't emphasize enough, how much time Ron spent calculating on our behalf, or the importance of his information and advice on the eventual aircraft loading and performance. *On the test flights, I also discovered just how uncomfortable we were going to be when we both got in that cramped cabin together – but there was no turning back now.*

The overhauled engine cylinders performed well, and the oil burn was now well below the burn required for a safe ocean crossing. But there was still one old minor problem that continued to plague the right engine. When taxiing in from the runway, after a long hot flight, the right engine had a tendency to quit at idle, indicating a possible weak engine–driven fuel pump. I decided not to take a chance, and had the pump removed and sent to the overhaul shop for testing. The shop never tested the pump as requested. They overhauled it, without knowing for certain whether it needed an overhaul or not. I wasn't very happy about this, but it was nearly time to leave. I felt that it couldn't hurt to know that the pump was as good as new again, so I had it reinstalled. The mechanics serviced the spark plugs and filters again, and declared the aircraft ready for the trip.

Navigation

There were more maps and charts required for the trip than could be carried in the cabin, so we stored those we would not be using for the next few days in the nose of the plane. The route was carefully plotted on the charts in use and a careful record of our actual progress kept during each flight. We had a hand–held computer, which gave us the course to fly, after we entered the forecast winds and the latitudes and longitudes for the points of origin and destination. We used this for determining our dead reckoning course, which is what you must fly, unless there is definite information to the contrary.

We carried three forms of long range radio navigation. The first was our new Apollo Loran C. Second was our King KR87 Automatic Direction Finder and its KR86 backup unit. (This instrument points at the signal source and you simply follow the needle towards it.) We obtained our third navigational radio from the Southern Cross Ferry Company in California. It was a Magnavox Satellite Navigator, modified for aviation use, and it provided us with a location fix approximately every hour when appropriate satellites passed by above the horizon. In the picture of the aircraft cabin, the Satnav is the rectangular box sitting on the edge of the pilot's seat, where we have removed the arm rest to provide the necessary space. Since the Loran C signal is not available everywhere, this Magnavox unit provided us with our position fixes when no other information was available, and provided us with a cross check when it was.

Communication

The normal VHF radios used throughout this continent do not have sufficient range for use far out over the water. A combination of low transmitter power and the inability of VHF signals to follow the curvature of the earth limits their range. Before reaching one hundred miles out to sea, pilots are required to establish communication on an HF (High Frequency) long range radio before they can obtain clearance to proceed farther. The clearance then specifies that a position report must be called in every hour. For the first half of the trip, the pilot calls the San Francisco AIRINC facility and then switches over to Honolulu AIRINC for the second half. I purchased an HF set from the Globe Aero Ferry company in Florida and mounted it on top of the aluminum tanks behind the pilots. There was six inches of room above the tanks and the radio was five inches high – another close fit. The Globe people use this set on all their ferry flights – so once again we were dealing with a proven product.

I knew that it was going to be next to impossible to get a radio serviced in most places along the route. Because of this, I carried a spare VHF communication radio under one seat. Under the other seat, I had a portable emergency battery pack in case my electrics failed. Wrapped in waterproof plastic, and attached to the life raft with a cord, was a hand held, battery powered VHF radio. It was intended for use in the event that we had to ditch in the water, or it could be unwrapped and used from the aeroplane if all the other radios should fail.

Survival

Obviously our best chance for survival was to keep the aero-plane in the air. *If we were to lose one engine in the early part of one of the first two long legs, we would be too heavy to stay airborne on the other engine for long.* The best we could hope for was a controlled descent on the one good engine. We did, however, have two or three actions we could take to prolong the descent in the first half of the flight and possibly even remain airborne in the second half. In the event of an engine failure, we would immediately add full tur-bocharging to the good engine. It might be hard on the engine, but I would rather the engine suffer than me.

Next, we would start draining the gas from one of our tanks, out through a dump valve and hose I had the tank installers place through the belly of the fuselage in the name of my wife and children. I also had a hunting knife handy to cut the rubber line from the other ferry tank and let its fuel run out through holes in the floor. There was a faint hope that some, or all of these measures, would keep us in the air or buy us time, before ditching in the ocean.

Approximately one third of our flights, however, were to take place over land. I had a small *land* emergency kit stored in the nose since there was no room in the cabin. On land, we could eventually get to this survival kit – if we survived the crash landing!

Maintenance

The whole flight of 26,000 miles was calculated to take approximately 150 flying hours. Since the aircraft engines should be serviced every 50 hours, I selected Singapore and Geneva, Switzerland for my maintenance. Tal had had his plane serviced in Geneva two years before during the Transatlantic Air Rally, and Singapore was the most developed country I could find near the first 50 hour mark. These two service stops also provided the advantage of heading into the third world, and home across the North Atlantic, with freshly serviced aeroplanes. I wrote various maintenance shops in Singapore several months ahead of departure. I eventually selected the Singapore Flying Club at the Seletar Air Force Base, because they previously had a Twin Comanche in their fleet, and their head mechanic was familiar with them. He advised me of a few gaskets and miscellaneous parts which were not easily available in Singapore and suggested we bring them along. Fortunately, they were small and light and we stored them in the nose with the charts and survival kit.

After months of planning, and considerable expense, my aeroplane was in perfect condition and ready for the longest flight of its life – *or so I thought!*

9

The Ultimate Challenge

MURPHY'S LAW

"Whatever can go wrong, will go wrong!"

I was destined to face the harsh reality of this law many times during the next eleven days.

Jim and I were blessed with a beautiful clear morning for our flight to Oakland. A number of friends and relatives gathered at the airport for a Bon Voyage along with the local media and photographers. At Oakland, the auxiliary tanks would be connected into our fuel system and, with the first morning tailwind, we would be up and away for our most critical leg – Hawaii!

My first premonition that all was not well occurred before we even climbed aboard. I noticed a small pool of oil under the right engine – impossible, but there it was! The engines had been checked, re-checked and declared perfect. We said our "Good Byes" and took off – but not for Oakland. We circled around and landed at the satellite airport, where all our preparatory maintenance had been performed. By noon the leak was located, repaired and pronounced airworthy. We took off again, this time without fanfare, but with high hopes that our mechanical problems were resolved. Was it an ill omen? I had arranged with Victor Koss, our

Optimistic second departure for Oakland. Wearing flight suits from Transatlantic Air Rally with "Woolworth" captain's stripes.

tanker in Oakland, that we would be waiting on his tarmac when he came to work the following morning. Our delayed departure necessitated flying over the mountains at night, but this was not a problem as Jim and I had flown together at night many times.

We fueled up at the half way point just before dark and started across the mountains via Salt Lake City for Oakland. *As we approached Ogden, Utah, one engine started banging and misfiring.* It was still developing partial power, but there was no way we were going to continue over the mountains at night on one and a half engines. We requested a diversion to Salt Lake City and landed there around eleven o'clock at night.

I was surprised to find that mechanics were working there on a night shift and enlisted one of them to help us. When he took off the engine cover, he found that one of the spark plug wires had fallen completely off its plug and was grounding on the engine frame. I requested a complete check of all the spark plug wires. The mechanic found one more lead ready to fall off and a number of others loose – on both engines. **I think if we had tried to continue on to Oakland we might well have lost both engines, with probable deadly results!**

The mechanic secured all the leads, and for reassurance, I double checked them myself. By that time, it was after midnight, so Jim and I went to a nearby hotel for the night. Day 1 had been a disaster, and my confidence was shaken. Imagine, facing engine breakdown after all my months of careful planning. Our tanker in Oakland would just have to wait, because we had had enough excitement for one day.

Victor Koss with pictures of planes he has tanked in the past few years for ferry flights across the Pacific Ocean. His Motto – ''The only time you can have too much fuel is when you're on fire.''

Early the next morning, we headed for Oakland with both engines purring as they should. Victor Koss was waiting impatiently for us and immediately started hooking up the auxiliary tanks. When ferry tanks are installed, a test flight has to be made before the Federal Aviation Authority inspectors will sign the aircraft out for its long overwater flight. The purpose of the test flight is to ensure that the fuel flows properly from the extra cabin tanks, even when they contain just a few gallons each. I had ten gallons put in each new tank, and we took off toward San Francisco and the ocean.

We were just levelling off at three thousand feet when the right engine suddenly lost power and very nearly quit. The fuel-flow gauge indicated that it was not getting the fuel it required, so we turned on the auxiliary electric pump for that side. Partial power was restored, and we radioed for an immediate return to the airport. This time my confidence in the aeroplane was really shattered!. **If we had tried to take off that day with our full load of**

Pacific fuel, my aeroplane would now be at the bottom of San Francisco bay! I am not sure where Jim and I would be.

The broken engine–driven fuel pump, showing its sheared drive shaft.

Leroy, a mechanic we were going to get to know and respect, found that the cursed little fuel pump, which had just been overhauled nine flying hours earlier, had seized and its drive shaft had sheared off. If only they had tested it back home as I had requested. Perhaps it hadn't required overhauling in the first place. Perhaps, if it had NEVER been touched – we wouldn't be in this mess.

During the next couple of days, we found out that the problem was even greater than any of us could have imagined. That pesky fuel pump, before it had seized completely and broken, had been self–destructing and contaminating the entire right engine fuel system with black graphite and metal shavings. It was therefore necessary to dismantle and clean the entire fuel system. The fuel metering device, the fuel distributor, and of course the broken pump, all had to be overhauled at a certified shop before we could try the engine again.

Fortunately, Oakland is replete with aviation facilities and one of their certified accessory overhaul shops gave us priority service. The repair still took several days. **In the light of the way that all my careful planning was coming unglued, I spent many anxious hours pondering the advisability of pursuing this adventure.**

While Tal and I waited patiently for my repairs to be made, Jim and Ken toured San Francisco. I managed to tear myself away from the Oakland airport for one day, and we all attempted to forget our troubles in the wine-tasting rooms of the Napa Valley vineyards.

During my life I have often heard that there is some good in every situation – if you look for it. I couldn't imagine what good could possibly come from the confinement to the Oakland Airport that Murphy's Law had forced upon me – but it was there that I met George.

Pilots are a friendly lot. As they sit in airport lounges waiting for better weather or aircraft to be repaired, conversations don't gradually commence – they literally spring up. I met many interesting people during my days at the airport, but one man stands out. He was a real swashbuckling adventurer named George Sigler.

George lived with his wife and children in Texas, where he worked part time in the real estate business. However, he was not often home for any length of time. He had served with the U.S. Navy flying jets from aircraft carriers and was still with the Naval Air Reserve. In his spare time, he ferried aeroplanes around the world.

In 1974 he designed a kit for survival at sea. Before he began marketing it, he and a friend set themselves adrift on a 2,600 mile Pacific voyage in a fifteen foot raft with only his survival kit to support them. On their second day out, the raft went stern over bow and turned over in high seas and heavy winds. They lost their camera equipment, food supplements, four cans of orange juice, clothing, a one-man life raft and other items. However, they hung on to the basics of his survival kit and managed to get back into the raft again and continue.

After forty days at sea without food, they became weak. They worried about whether they would have the strength to get their raft right-side-up if it swamped again in a storm or if it was bumped by a whale. Luckily, it didn't overturn again. One day they caught five, twenty-five pound fish known as Mahi-Mahi. When two birds landed on their raft one night, George said "we just snuck up on 'em and grabbed 'em." When asked what kind of birds they were George replied "I don't know one kind of seabird from another."

The two men got within eighty miles of the island of Oahu, Hawaii, but were unable to make a landfall. The navy had been tracking them and requested that they allow themselves to be picked up at sea, so that doctors could test the two men's physical condition at Pearl Harbor in Honolulu. George and his friend reluctantly agreed. *Adrift for fifty-six days, George had lost fifty-one pounds and his friend had lost forty-seven. Each man now weighed less than 130 pounds. That's what I call testing your product before putting it on the market!*

One of George's other interesting experiences was more directly related to what we were about to attempt ourselves. Thirty days before we met George, he was flying a used Cessna 310 twin engine aeroplane from Oakland to New Zealand with the Owner aboard as his co-pilot. Roughly 500 miles past Hawaii, one engine sprang an oil leak, ran out of oil and seized. In an attempt to keep the aircraft in the air on one engine, he cut the rubber fuel lines to the ferry tanks in the cabin. Fuel ran all over the floor, around their feet and out some holes in the floor of the plane. (That's where I learned that trick I mentioned in the last chapter).

Unfortunately, George's good engine was not turbocharged, and he couldn't get rid of enough fuel before he reached the water, so he was forced to ditch. He did have time, however, to contact Honolulu and tell them of his predicament before he hit the water. George and his passenger made it safely into their small raft. They were too far from land for a Helicopter rescue, so a long range Hercules rescue aircraft dropped them a pair of thirty-man life rafts joined together by a long rope. The rafts were dropped in front of them so they would drift toward the rope somewhere between the rafts and then pull themselves toward the nearest one. The next day, they were picked up by a Japanese fishing vessel which had altered its course to rescue them. Following three days of unexpected nonstop Sushi aboard that welcome little vessel, they were safely back in Honolulu. *When I met him, a month later, he was back in Oakland kicking another set of tires and preparing for another ferry flight to New Zealand.*

When a pilot with those credentials tells you something about ocean flying, you listen. One piece of advice he had for us was to figure out what heading we were going to fly for those long distances over water and "Stick To It!" If the wind appeared to be different than forecast, a heading change of only one or two degrees was plenty. You can easily get too far off course for your fuel reserves if you start changing course too drastically or too often en route. Jim and I made a mental note of that and stuck to it!

You don't meet people like George, sitting at home in your living room!

Eventually, my overhauled aircraft parts were returned and placed back on the right engine – which now had the cleanest fuel system imaginable. We ran the engine up and it sounded great. Jim got in the pilot's seat for another attempt at the mandatory fuel-flow test flight and began his engine run–up check. First he checked the right engine. HALLELUJAH! It was perfect. Then he pushed the throttle for the left engine. There should have been nothing to worry about on this side. After all, the left engine had NEVER given me any problem. But Murphy was still hiding some-where in that aeroplane!

The aeroplane began to shudder and the dash board started shaking so wildly Jim was afraid it would damage the instruments. Leroy's trained

The Golden Boy's left engine awaiting return of overhauled cylinder at Oakland.

ear brought him running from the hangar, and I nearly cried. One of the cylinders, freshly overhauled just sixty flying hours ago, had failed! It was five o'clock Friday afternoon, and I could visualize us all here for another week, while we found someone to overhaul this cylinder again. Tal's patience, which had been exemplary to this point, was exhausted. He began to talk of taking his co–pilot Ken on a tour of the United States, instead of around the world.

But Leroy had a friend. This friend ran a certified engine shop at a small airport across the bay. Leroy regularly had all his cylinder work done there. He called his friend, who agreed to come in Saturday morning and repair the cylinder himself, while I waited. Leroy said that he too would come in to work, with a mechanic, at noon Saturday and put the engine back together. This gave all our spirits a lift. To cut the time to a minimum, Tal offered to fly me across the bay and back, with my cylinder. *What a wonderful group of people! They knew the effort and expense we had invested to this point and genuinely wanted to help us get our adventure finally underway.*

Saturday afternoon, around five o'clock, the left engine was back together and running. It seemed too good to be true. Everything was finally working again. But could we depend on it? Jim and I had agreed that we couldn't trust our lives to this machine until we were certain that Murphy was still not lurking onboard. We made a pact with each other. On Sunday morning we would fly up and down the California coast, within range of land, for six hours. If either engine did not perform as it should, we would call the whole adventure off and return home. If everything worked satisfactorily we would head for Honolulu the following morning – provided we had a tailwind.

Statistically, we could expect a tailwind one day out of three. The wind had been between thirteen and sixteen knots in our favor for the past three days in a row. Could it possibly continue for another day or two? That problem would have to wait until we were certain we could go at all!

Sunday morning, I topped up both engines with just over eight quarts of oil. I put a few extra gallons of gas in each ferry tank for testing purposes (but not so much that we couldn't fly on one engine if we had to). I bought a couple of sandwiches and filled my thermos with coffee. With Tal, Ken and Leroy cheering us on, Jim and I climbed into the plane and took off. For the first hour we ran the engines hard, because we had to seat the piston rings in the newly overhauled cylinder. Then we throttled back to 2,200 RPM and twenty-two inches of manifold pressure on each engine. These were the settings we planned to use for fuel economy over the ocean the next day. The sound of those two smooth running engines was music to my ears. All systems performed perfectly.

I transferred fuel from both ferry tanks to our main wing tanks according to plan. It was simple and worked well. The fuel computers, exhaust gas temperatures and cylinder head temperatures all read normal. Jim and I settled down to see how well we were going to survive in our cramped quarters for the allotted six hours. The worst period for me came at about four and a half hours. After that I seemed to adjust – or perhaps I just became numb. One thing that seemed to help was to take my shoes off and stretch my toes up in behind the rudder pedals periodically. This provided my six foot, two inch frame with another three or four inches extension of my legs and let me flex my knee joints a few degrees. When we landed at the end of the six hours we were both cautiously optimistic. Only one major question remained. Had the rings on the rebuilt cylinder seated properly so that it was not burning oil?

It was Sunday afternoon when we landed. The first person to reach the plane was Leroy. He checked the oil in both engines. Both sides had burned the same – one quart in six hours. That calculated to two and a half quarts of oil burned during the proposed fifteen hours to Honolulu, which would leave us with over five quarts in each engine on arrival. That was more than adequate. Leroy then uncowled both engines to look for oil leaks or any signs of trouble. There were none. Everything was clean and dry. We were ready at last!

We then converged on the weather office and were handed the fresh forecast for Monday morning. I could hardly believe my eyes. They were still forecasting a nine knot average tailwind for our course to Hawaii. They were also forecasting a cloud cover for San Francisco but clear out over the ocean. Good enough! No stopping the rushing river now! We would go!

And we would leave Murphy behind us, where he belonged.

10

The Ultimate Challenge

FLYING THE PACIFIC

On Monday, July 13th, 1987, Jim and I rose to the sound of our alarm clock at 4:00 AM. At 4:30 we were off to the all night coffee shop for toast and coffee. There, we met with Tal and Ken, to make a final check of our sequential navigational calculations for the seven position fixes we would be passing, over the Pacific ocean.

The "Professional Pilot" magazine in a recent article* states, "The most common single reason for gross navigational errors, in making an oceanic crossing, is not equipment malfunction but errors in programming (or loading) the flight plan into the system." I couldn't agree more! *As we checked our figures for the ocean fixes, we suddenly realized that all of the calculations we had made on our hand–held Nav Gem navigational computers were wrong.* We had programmed the magnetic variations as a plus factor instead of a minus. It took an hour at the breakfast booth to correct all the figures and agree on them before we went to the airport.

I checked over the plane and had it gassed up. I had waited to fuel in the morning, because I didn't want the undercarriage supporting the excess fuel weight overnight. The people at Kaiser Air, from whom we had purchased all our fuel, gave us each a bottle of wine and a loaf of authentic San Francisco sourdough bread as a

*"Making a Crossing" by Allan Schwab, page 68, August, 1988 issue.

momento of our unexpected prolonged stay in the San Francisco Bay area. We were sorry to leave them, for they had become our friends and supporters of our adventure.

Leroy (centre) with both crews after successful six hour test flight.

We flight planned for 6000 feet, the minimum allowable altitude for the flight, and taxied to Oakland's longest runway for takeoff. An hour and a half later than planned, with 10,000 feet of runway in front of us, I pre–set the turbochargers for an extra half inch of boost and Jim pushed the throttles forward. As we accelerated down the runway, I glanced to my side and saw two familiar figures waving and wishing us luck. It was Victor Koss, our tanking specialist, and good old Leroy, our faithful mechanic. With 15 degrees of flap, the plane struggled into the air at the 3000 foot marker. Up came the landing gear, and we started climbing into the typical Bay Area early morning stratus cloud cover. We entered the cloud at 800 feet and locked our eyes onto the instruments. The aeroplane was sluggish, as my previous tests with water in the ferry tanks had indicated it would be, but at least we were climbing.

We pulled out on top of the cloud at about 3000 feet and were surprised to see a tower sticking up into the clear blue sky. It was obviously mounted on top of a bay area mountain, which remained concealed just below the top of the stratus cloud. I kept anxiously looking back at that tower. It represented, as it poked up through the cloud in isolation, our last sight of a land–based object for many hours. Ordinarily I might not have felt so squeamish, but the mechanical failures of the past 10 days had unnerved me. I realized now how frail these little machines were. **I hoped I wasn't getting my son into something we couldn't get out of.**

A couple of minutes later, Tal popped up out of the cloud behind us somewhere. The controllers vectored him toward us until we made visual contact with each other. Seeing our friends beside us made me feel better! We were then cleared en route to the first check point out over the ocean as a two–aeroplane formation "flight." That meant that Jim and I were to do the radio work with the controllers and the other plane was to stay in sight of us and just listen–in to all the conversations.

Initially, we never saw any water at all because of the cloud below us. *It was exciting to think of ourselves in that little plane out over the Pacific Ocean. I didn't put in my ear plugs at first because I loved hearing the sound of those two engines, on which so much depended. If one*

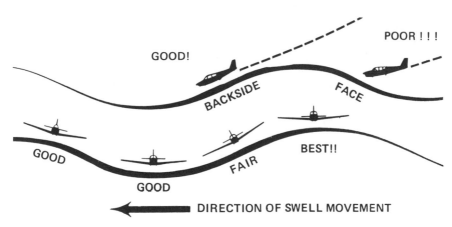

Ditching procedures in a rolling sea.

of them should falter this early in the flight, we were going for a swim. The life raft was under my knees, and Jim and I each wore our inflatable life vests. George had lectured us at length on the best way to ditch a plane in the swells of a rolling sea, should it become necessary. But we hoped never to make use of his instructions..

For the first four hours, it was impossible to fly the plane on autopilot. As Victor Koss and the FAA inspector had both advised us, the weight and balance at this loading was truly at the outer edge of the "envelope." Therefore the autopilot could not be depended upon to hold the plan level. Jim became our autopilot, and it took his full concentration to perform that function. At first it was like flying a teeter-totter. We throttled back to the planned power settings for economy cruise, and the aeroplanes' performance was exactly as predicted. I leaned out the fuel flow to six and one half gallons per hour on each side, and got out the camera to record the beauty of the moment. Soon the clouds were behind us. and there was nothing but blue sky and blue water as far as the eye could see.

Tal and I stayed in sight of each other, and we took pictures of each other's aeroplanes. We flew on the left, then on the right, then above and below, speeded up a little and slowed down again. It was great company to have that other aeroplane along for this fifteen hour flight and to have another crew to converse with. I had been told by several people before we left, that if we got lost on the way to Honolulu, all we had to do was look up or down for guidance. Below us, we were supposed to see freighters plying the shipping lanes to Hawaii. Above, there should be contrails from the many jets full of tourists flying back and forth to the mainland. Alas, all any of us saw was each other. I was glad we weren't lost!

The HF radio in my plane worked well for about 700 miles. *After that, I was never able to talk to San Francisco again.* I had been requested to report the position of our two-aeroplane "flight" every hour. Once again, I made use of some advice I had picked up in the "hangar talk" during my forced confinement at the Oakland airport. I called for assistance in passing my report on the international emergency frequency 121.5 MHZ. I knew that all airline jets keep one of their radios tuned to that frequency while they are out over the ocean, and that their pilots are not overly busy in level flight unless the weather is bad. The captain of an American Airlines jet heard me and was pleased to assist by relaying my position report back to San Francisco and confirming its receipt. I repeated this procedure hourly, throughout the middle third of the route, until we got close to Hawaii. Then we were once again within radio range ourselves. Tal and I were both concerned about the limited range of our HF radios, since they should have been good for several times the distance we were getting. I resolved to try and solve the problem when I got to Hawaii. The engines were still running well, and that was the most important issue right now.

Our Apollo Loran C radios surprised us the other way. The books on the subject indicate a large area, near the middle of our route, where there is no satisfactory signal. Both aeroplanes were able to receive dependable latitude and longitude readings essentially all the way to Hawaii, except for perhaps fifty miles. Every hour we cross-checked the readings on our Loran C radios with our Satellite Navigational receivers and with each other. They never differed by more than one degree. *Thus, we were able to confirm our position at all times from four separate sources. It was a great comfort, because all we could see in every direction was water, water and more water.*

However, that's about all the comfort there was. My shoes were off, and my toes were up behind the rudder pedals again. Every few minutes, I shifted a little from side to side. I pumped up the air bag in the seat covers we had been given, to support the small of my back. Awhile later, I let the air out – just so I could have something to do. We ate our sandwiches in stages, spreading our snack times out as much as possible. I drank some orange juice and had a coke. I sat upright for awhile and then slouched for a change. Many, many times we looked at our watches. The time went slowly, like a boring movie which never seems to end. I thought how much nicer this trip was going to be when the first two long flights were behind us.

When people talk to me about this portion of the flight, they invariably attempt to find some polite way to enquire about our bathroom facilities. We carried a series of plastic bottles, tested ahead of time for leakage, in a discreet cloth bag so that we could carry them into the terminal washroom at our destinations. That was easy – I have been doing that for years. The other possible problem took more thought. My solution was to purchase two rectangular refrigerator dishes, three inches high, with tight fitting press-down lids. Because of space limitations, these containers had to do double duty. I filled them with a number of items, which I hoped we would also never need in flight, such as a spare microphone, air sick bags, flashlight batteries etc. and stored one under each seat. The good news is that we never needed them on the entire trip. *The amazing news is, that all the way to Hawaii, Jim never used the bottles either.* But then, he is a lot younger than I am.

My bookkeeping chores on the flight included a careful record of our fuel consumption. We had the six regular wing tanks and the two large ferry tanks in the cabin. As Victor Koss had suggested, and the FAA inspector in Oakland had confirmed, the safest way to manage the fuel was to keep the engines running off our largest wing tanks and to fill these periodically from the ferry tanks. Even this simple system provided some excitement. Sometimes, when we turned the ferry tank valves either on or off, an air bubble seemed to enter the line and go through the engine along with the gas. This caused a momentary abrupt change in the engine performance. It gave us quite a scare the first time it happened. We soon learned to do one engine at a time and to turn on our electric boost pumps before we laid a hand on the ferry tank fuel valves. I knew the engine wasn't going to quit, but I couldn't stop that shot of adrenaline from going through my system each time the engine hesitated.

About two thirds of the way to Hawaii, we encountered patches of cumulus cloud which covered about half of the sky. We could still see the water below and the blue sky above. Gradually the cloud thickened as we approached the islands. We cancelled our combined "flight" status and became separate aeroplanes to the controllers in Honolulu. *The clouds thickened and darkened as we approached the islands. Eventually we were back on instruments. The skies turned from grey to black and there was thunder and lightning all around us.* Because we had been late taking off in Oakland, it was now well past sunset. The controllers vectored us around Diamond Head and lined us up for an instrument approach to the Honolulu International airport runway and down we came. Squeak, squeak, squeak. Three wheels safely on the ground – we had made it! I opened the door and there were two more squeaks – my knees straightening out as I emerged from our capsule. It felt good to take my feet out from under those rudder pedals and place them once again on solid ground.

Two or three minutes behind us, Tal and Ken broke out of the cloud for their landing, and right behind them was good old

George Sigler. He had taken off in a larger and faster Cessna 402 about three hours behind us and had gained back all that time en route. George showed us where we could get a twelve cent per gallon discount on gas, *now that we were fully qualified ferry pilots,* and we all checked into a nearby Holiday Inn at Air Crew rates. We were tired and stiff but quite pleased with ourselves. The first obstacle had been beaten. There was much more to come, but I was confident now that we could handle it.

In the morning, we all returned to the aircraft to check them over in the daylight. We had burned only two quarts of oil in the right engine and slightly less in the left. Both engines looked clean and dry. They couldn't have looked better! *I mentally kissed them both.* Tal's engines also looked good, and we turned our attention to the disappointing HF radios. George, of course, had the solution. The wire antennae was too short and strung in too sharp a ''V.'' George, naturally, had an extra coil of wire. We disconnected the antennae from the engine nacelle and strung it out wider and further to the wing tip. George said it might be in our way a little, getting in and out of the plane, but it should work better – and it did. I was able to talk to controllers two thousand miles away for the remainder of the trip.

Nuclear powered submarine, S.S. Omaha, berthed in Pearl Harbor for refit.

For entertainment during our one day visit to Honolulu, George suggested we rent a car and do three things. First we picked up, from the FAA, a copy of the cassette tape containing all the radio transmissions George had made to the controllers a few weeks previous, during his controlled descent into the ocean. Second, we listened to it in the car as we drove for lunch to the Officers' Club in Pearl Harbor. And finally, after lunch, George used his Naval reserve identification to arrange a tour through a nuclear powered submarine. The SS Omaha was in Pearl taking on supplies for further active duty. The five of us spent a most interesting two hours aboard, touring all of the unclassified facilities, and learned a great deal about submarines. One item of special interest to our group was that Navy submarines used the same Magnavox satellite navigator we were using in our aeroplanes. If it was good enough to provide navigational back-up for the U.S. Navy – then it was certainly good enough for us.

George Sigler in Honolulu just before he left us for New Zealand via Samoa.

The next morning, George was first to take off at about 6:45 AM, headed for Samoa and New Zealand. We never saw him again, but I am sure he is still regularly flying the Pacific. I know that there was a Cessna 310, destined for Australia, all tanked up and waiting for him when he returned to Oakland. Tal and I took off as a "flight" a few minutes later. It was a beautiful clear morning. We were soon playing leap frog with each other again as we headed for Majuro in the Marshall Islands. This second Pacific flight was almost as long as the first, but it did have one safety factor – an airport on a coral atoll, called Johnson Island, about 500 miles from Honolulu. The island is an American military nerve-gas disposal center and is off-limits to all civilian aircraft – except in the case of a declared emergency. Its navigational beacon does provide a positive ADF fix, however, and is a great source of comfort to all planes passing that way.

Johnson Island, the only island between Hawaii and the Marshall Islands.

Once again, we had our four navigational radios cross-checking each other and all was going well – until we passed over Johnson Island. At that point, Tal's gyro compass became undependable and his Loran C malfunctioned. Instead of following us outbound from Johnson Island on the correct course, his radios led him to believe he should be headed farther North. After much discussion, *Tal decided that he was not comfortable continuing with his faulty avionics, declared an emergency, and landed on the island.* Since we had no emergency, Jim and I decided to continue. Before we separated, we agreed to meet again, somewhere among the next few planned stops, after he had his radios repaired back in Hono-lulu.

When we left Tal at Johnson Island, it was Wednesday. A couple of hours later it suddenly was Thursday. We had crossed the international date line! At this point our Loran C signal faded out and there would be no more signal generating stations along our route until we reached Saudi Arabia. This was the portion of the trip where the Satellite Navigator radio earned its keep with a position fix every hour or so. Our HF radio was now functioning well. We could communicate across two thousand miles. Also we still had the basic tool of ocean flying, ''Dead Reckoning,'' with which to work. Jim never changed his course setting for over eight hours – just as George had suggested. When we finally came within range of the Majuro beacon, about 300 miles out, we required less than a five degree correction to head directly over the airport.

A typical small, uninhabited, Pacific Ocean Atoll.

We arrived after dark because of being nearly an hour late taking off. **Once again, about fifty miles out we ran into cloud, rain, thunder and lightning. Our plane was pitched and tossed around, violently at times, and I was glad that we had burned off**

the major portion of our fuel load. Otherwise, the turbulence might have been too much for the airframe.

The instrument approach at Majuro is only a simple cloud–breaking procedure. All the training Jim and I ever had was called into play – flying through a violent rainstorm at night, into an island runway, in the middle of the ocean, that we had never seen before. There were no options of diverting to an airport with better weather. And we both were suffering from the fatigue of spending over 14 hours in a noisy cramped cockpit!

Majuro Atoll in the Marshall Islands. Home to 12,000 people.

Majuro is also an atoll, only about 200 yards wide and 26 circular miles long. The town is at one end of the island and the airport is about 8 miles away, down the only road. We rode into town with an airport employee in his half–ton truck. The three of us filled the tiny cab, so our bags stayed out in the rain. The truck stalled at least ten times going through deep puddles of water. When we finally arrived at the little eighteen room hotel, we were told that all the rooms were taken. George had told us that he stayed there often and that, if we had any trouble, we should mention his name. Standing at the front desk soaking wet, *I told the clerk that George had sent us, and magically, they moved someone out of one of the rooms, cleaned it up, and gave it to us.*

By morning, the rain had stopped and we went across the street for breakfast at the Likrok Cafe. We went into the cafe and sat down. The waitress came over and sat down at our table with us. She gave us a big smile and asked what we would like to have. I pointed to a number of things on the menu, including coffee. She said we couldn't have any of them. This confused us for awhile, until we discovered that the power was off and cooking very limited. The only choice we had was between Beef or Chicken Ramen, which had been heated on a gas stove. Jim and I both ordered the Chicken Ramen. It turned out to be noodles, vegetables, and several pieces of chicken, with the skin still on, boiled together in a kind of stew. It wasn't bad!

Two other gentlemen were sitting at tables near a window, unconcernedly reading their papers. They didn't appear to either be eating or ordering anything. Just as we finished our breakfast, the lights came on, and they placed their orders. They didn't order Ramen: they had eggs, toast and coffee.

After breakfast, we caught a cab to the airport. Since there is only one road, the cabs are regular small cars which start at one end of the island and travel to the other. Then they turn around and go back. The fare, within the general town limits, was thirty cents. You could get in anywhere and get out anywhere, the distance was not important. As long as there was an empty seat in the cab it would stop for you. If it was full, the driver tooted his horn as he drove by.

At the airport, we talked to Dave Gamanche, the head mechanic for the Micronesian Airline that services the Marshall Islands. He turned out to be a displaced Canadian from our home town of Winnipeg. When he had completed his regular work, he helped us remove one ferry tank from the cabin and re-connect the other into the fuel system. We also centered the remaining tank and moved it back about eight inches. The aeroplane seats could now travel back and forth and the seat backs reclined as the manufacturer had intended them to do. *We had our creature comforts back, and the very long flights were over.* We could still carry fuel for about twelve hours, but our average flights from here on were going to be half of that, or less.

Majuro doesn't have very much going for it. The 12,000 people living on that ring of coral reef, support themselves off copra, some

Our rear cabin area after one ferry tank has been removed and the remaining tank moved back to permit full movement of cockpit seats.

fishing, a U.S. firing range and tourism. The Marshalls were controlled by the Japanese until the end of World War II, when they became a U.S. trust territory. The trust ended in 1981, but the islands remain almost totally dependent on American support. We left a few dollars of further support on Majuro and made plans to leave for Truk Island, Micronesia and some scuba diving.

11

The Ultimate Challenge

THE TRUK LAGOON

We now had passed the point of "No Return". With one gas tank removed, we no longer had sufficient fuel to return to North America, except by continuing on via the South Pacific, the Third World, Europe and the North Atlantic. Our next stop, Truk, was located about eleven hundred miles due West of Majuro. Our estimated flying time for this flight was eight hours. Not only was this just slightly more than half the distance we had been flying recently, but we were going to be able to land after five and a half hours for gas. There were now several choices for our fuel stops. We chose the island of Ponape.

I had been told that fuel is available only in multiples of fifty-five gallon drums on Truk. Pilots object to buying gas from a previously opened drum, as it might be contaminated with water or other impurities. The solution was to land at Ponape and fill up the tanks to the point where we would require one complete additional drum after flying the remaining two and a half hours to Truk. This would give us nearly full tanks, without any wastage, when we left Truk for New Guinea.

Flying through light rain and cloud all the way to Ponape, we missed the bright sunshine experienced on our first two long flights. However, we felt the absence of our companions even more. I also missed seeing that other little aeroplane off our wing-tip, for it had been our safety net until now. *It was lonely out there over the Pacific, with no one to chatter at.* I still had to make our hourly position reports, but these were formal conversations. Many times Jim and I talked about how much we hoped Tal and Ken would be able to get their radios fixed and catch up with us at the Truk Lagoon, or shortly thereafter.

Ponape had a good 6,000 foot asphalt runway, but the airport was unattended except for one young lad. He explained that the airport was run by a missionary named Harvey Pace. We telephoned Harvey and he came right out to the airport. He is a very unusual person, and leads an interesting life. Harvey is a pilot as well as a missionary. He flies three aeroplanes, a King Air, an Aero Commander and a Beech 18. He told us the story of a medical epidemic that occurred on one of the Caroline Islands, some distance away. There was no landing strip on the island, and the natives radioed that they needed antibiotics immediately. There was no time to wait for water transport. Harvey rigged some bedsheets into home-made parachutes, flew over their island, and dropped them their life-saving supplies. A week later the natives radioed that all was now well.

At the Ponape airport, Harvey had on hand plenty of gas, an electric pump and four young helpers. He sold us exactly the number of gallons I calculated we would need, and at his cost. That is the one and only time in my life I ever bought aircraft gas at anyone's cost. He said he was in the business of helping people – not making money from them. His four young assistants also refused my offer of payment for their help. That behaviour said a lot for the influence of Harvey and his teachings, on the young people of Ponape. On the phone, the local forecaster told Jim that the weather was improving toward Truk, so we left Harvey and his lovely island behind us.

Two and a half hours later we were in Truk. We decided to check into the best hotel on the island, the Continental Hotel. It is owned by Continental Airways, which services most of the islands in this part of the world under the name ''Air Mike'' for Air Micronosia. We had an excellent, spacious room with modern plumbing and a view of the ocean. *That was lucky because, for the next 24 hours, Jim and I never left the room.*

Our problem must have originated either with that chicken Ramon we had for breakfast in Majuro or with the delicious glass of ice cold coconut drink we had at noon. In any event, the germs rode with us to Truk and then struck with a vengeance. I looked to Jim for the solution, because he had been assigned to bring the medical supplies. He didn't let me down. In his kit he had drugs to slow us down. We each took large doses and went back to bed, thankful we didn't have to fly the following morning.

The second morning, Jim was much better and went scuba diving on the sunken Japanese ship wrecks. After all, that is why we had included this lagoon in our route. I was much better but not well enough to trust myself in ninety feet of water. While Jim dove, I went to the airport and supervised the fueling of the plane and made sure that all was in readiness for departure. When Jim returned from his diving, we approached a local businessman about hiring a taxi for a tour of the island. He said there were no taxis available, but he would be pleased to be our tour guide.

The island of Truk and its sheltered coral lagoon was the forward staging area for the Japanese navy in the Pacific during World War II. In February of 1944 the Americans essentially executed a Pearl Harbor in reverse, when they sank some fifty Japanese ships with two carrier based raids on the lagoon. There would have been more ships inside that coral ring, if the Japanese had not spotted an American reconnaissance plane that was sent to look over the area one week before the raid. Admiral Yamamoto became suspicious and removed many of his war ships from the lagoon.

Truk has often been referred to as the "Gibraltar of the Pacific." During the raid, the American planes dropped 500 pound bombs on the communications center building. At least two direct hits barely put a dent in the roof, for it was made of reinforced concrete four feet thick. The Japanese had built a veritable fortress on the island. The buildings had doors and windows with heavy steel shutters. The entire island was ringed with eight inch guns pointing out through holes in the rocky hillsides. The hills still contain elaborate passageways and ammunition storage areas cut

Japanese Communications Centre building showing heavy steel shutters and four feet thick concrete roof.

into the rock. Our friend gave us a most interesting tour of the facilities.

As we drove around the island, he told us about the day the liquor referendum was called. It seems it caught most of the men

Drinking Island in Truk lagoon.

while they were out fishing. The women, who felt liquor was ruining the island's productivity, mounted a campaign and delivered a one hundred percent turn out for the vote. The result was a landslide victory for prohibition, and now all forms of liquor are forbidden on the island. *There is, however, another very small island, just offshore, that the vote did not cover. So every Saturday, the men row out to the little island, break open their cache of liquor, and proceed to drink as they had always done before the referendum.*

There are two positive results from all those ships sunk within that sandy lagoon. The first is that oceanographers know exactly what day the coral and marine life began attaching itself to the underwater hulls. They have been able to keep track of growth rates year by year, and have thus learned a lot about the genesis and evolution of new ocean reefs. Secondly, hundreds of tourists come to Truk every year to dive among the wrecks in 80 degree, relatively calm, shallow water.

The next morning, I was well enough to dive. Jim had requested ,the previous day, that the divemaster take him and the diving party to underwater ships that did not have aeroplanes in them. This was so we could all go to those wrecks with aeroplanes when I was feeling better. I was very appreciative of this arrangement, for all three of my dives ended up in or around an underwater Japanese aircraft.

It is customary in diving to do the deep dive first. My first dive was ninety feet down into the front hold of an aircraft supply ship – the "Fujikawa Maru." There, I climbed into the cockpit of one of the three Japanese Zeros stored in the hold. As I sat moving the controls, I could almost see and hear the bombing and sinking of the Zeros. It was difficult to believe that these aeroplanes had been underwater over forty–three years. On the way up I toured the deck of the ship. It was still littered with ammunition and guns. There were also dishes, kitchen utensils, and personal effects. **It was eerie!**

Fortunately there were no skeletons or bones. After the war, when tourists began to dive these wrecks, many underwater pictures were taken, and remnants of bodies could be seen. Some of these photos appeared in Japanese magazines. There was a public outcry from relatives, and the Japanese government spent a great deal of money recovering all of the skeletons from the ships in this lagoon.

The bones were gathered into a large funeral pyre on land in Truk and, after a formal Japanese memorial ceremony, were set ablaze.

Jim (left) and Don (right) diving Japanese ''Betty'' bomber resting in 30 feet of water in Truk lagoon.

We decompressed over lunch and then snorkeled around another Zero that had been shot down from the air. It now rested upside down in only fifteen feet of water. In the afternoon we dove a Japanese ''Betty Bomber'' which also had been shot down. This bomber had been built by ''Mitsubishi,'' the company from which we now buy television sets. It lay only thirty feet below the surface, so I was able to travel right through the fuselage into the cockpit. I passed by a bank of oxygen tanks, still in place, climbed into the pilot's seat and tried to visualize the nightmarish two days in 1944 that had produced all of this destruction.

That evening, at the hotel, I received a phone call from Tal. He was still in Honolulu but had received his repaired Loran C radio back from the U.S. and was leaving in the morning for Majuro. He advised that he would join up with us again the following day in Papua, New Guinea. That was great news!

In the morning, at breakfast, we met a crew of television photographers for the American Broadcasting Company. They were in Truk producing a documentary on life as it is in these islands, some forty years after the big raid. There was a Japanese machine gun mounted in firing position on a concrete pad on the hotel lawn. The ABC crew thought it would be an asset to their film to have us fly by while they took our picture passing across that old gunsight. This would illustrate that all is quiet now and that only small civilian aircraft now fly where fierce dogfights once took place. *We agreed and that's the way we left Truk – in a low, high speed, waterfront pass, with television cameras whirring beneath us.*

12

The Ultimate Challenge

THE SOUTH PACIFIC

We headed out over the water for another eight hours in the air. It was a beautiful day for a change, and our HF radio was working well. We called Honolulu and obtained our clearance for Port Moresby in Papua New Guinea, usually referred to as PNG.

When our satellite navigator box read latitude 00° 00' we were over the equator. Jim and I shook hands to acknowledge this new horizon. This was the first time we had been on the other side of the world together. For awhile, everything would be upside down for us.

The Honolulu controllers gave us the radio frequency for Port Moresby radio and bid us good-bye. We were never able to contact our new controllers on the frequencies we had received, so we returned to talk again with Hawaii. Honolulu assured us several times that they had informed the people at PNG of our arrival and then closed out our flight plan.

Jim and I were growing more complacent about ocean flying. We had developed renewed confidence in the aeroplane and in our ability to use our navigational equipment. Here we were, in the middle of nowhere, with no companion aircraft. We were on a seldom travelled route, and there would be no scheduled planes above us or ships below us. *We were probably in as vulnerable a position as we would ever be, and what were we doing? We were reading our National Geographic excerpts on Papua New Guinea! We were so relaxed that if others could have seen us then, they might have thought we both were back home sitting in our local public library.*

PNG is formally referred to as a "Nation In The Making". I feel a more accurate description is expressed in the real estate parlance, "Needs Work." PNG consists of the mainland plus six hundred islands. It has a population of three million, about ninety percent of whom are Nationals. The remainder are referred to as Expatriots. The main island is the second largest in the world, smaller only than Greenland. Over forty percent of the population live in the highlands, where they speak more than 700 different dialects – in fact one sixth of all the world's languages. The reason for this is they have lived in communities that were isolated from each other in the rugged mountain regions for centuries. There are no roads linking the villages with each other or with the cities. We read, however, that they have recently developed airstrips in a few of the remote areas. Jim and I decided that we would fly into one of these, if at all possible, for our PNG sightseeing day.

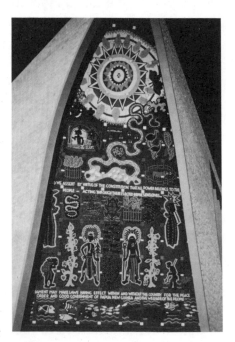

PNG Parliament Building face.

Papua was governed by the British, and New Guinea by the Germans, until the end of World War I. The Japanese controlled PNG from then until the end of World War II. Australia acted as caretaker until 1975, at which time PNG gained its independence. When this happened, the twenty–five thousand Australian civil servants were sent home and replaced by fifty thousand Nationals. The Expatriots were allowed to stay only until they had taught their job to a National. PNG built a new legislative building in an African motif with the following words emblazoned on its face: "And We Assert By Virtue Of The Constitution That All Power Belongs To The People." *Jim and I were destined to find out the full meaning of that word "ASSERT."*

Port Moresby, PNG.

We were headed for their capital city of Port Moresby which has about 120,000 inhabitants. As we approached the island, we tried desperately to establish a satisfactory radio contact. Twice I was able to talk to one of their National Airline captains. Each time, I was told that he had advised the authorities of our position and our proposed arrival. One of the captains relayed a message to me from a PNG controller requesting that I call their station at Madang on my HF radio, and I was given the frequency to use. There was no reply to my persistent calls. I couldn't understand it. Medang was only about a hundred miles away.

To check my radio performance, I called Hawaii, over two thousand miles away. They came in loud and clear. I again requested that they call PNG and advise them of my position and proposed arrival. I was told that they had done this, so I returned to the Madang frequency and continued calling – again without results. We reached the North coast of PNG and started climbing to sixteen thousand feet to cross the mountain range between us and Port Moresby. As we crossed the highest ridge, we were finally able to make contact on our regular VHF communication radio. We called the tower and requested permission for our descent and approach. *They asked "Who are you and where did you come from?" I couldn't believe it! I had received half a dozen different assurances that our arrival advice had been passed on to these people but the tower seemed to think we had just popped up, unannounced, from Mars.*

After we landed, the tower controller asked me to telephone a certain number but declined to say why. We parked beside several other small aeroplanes, opened our door and gratefully planted our feet once more on terra firma. Immediately, we could hear noise and laughter coming from a nearby building. The sign out front said "South Pacific Aero Club," so we headed toward it to make our phone call.

As we entered the building, we were greeted by their President, Stuart Thompson. Within five minutes of landing, we found ourselves with a beer in our hands and meeting members of the club. During this "happy hour," I tried several times to call the number given to me by the tower after we landed. It was always busy. After about three hours, I concluded that someone had left the receiver off the hook.

The flying club members were very interested in our world journey, and also with our proposed flight into a mountain airstrip, scheduled for the following morning. They selected Goroka as the most appropriate airstrip for us, provided us with the necessary local charts, and made arrangements for us to be met upon arrival. A University professor was to show us around the villages near the airstrip. The flight promised to be exactly what we had been hoping for, sitting in our flying library, back out over the Pacific – a chance to visit the rural native culture.

When evening came, Stuart Thompson found us a room in Port Moresby's newest Inn, appropriately called the Airport Motel. It had been open for about a month. Checking in took about an hour. The girl at the front desk had no idea, from her records or assorted papers, what beds were in any of the rooms. When we asked for a room with two beds, she would select an empty room and then send the bellhop up with the key to count the beds. Each trip took him about ten minutes. She did this one room at a time, until I suggested that she give the young man several sets of keys at a time and save him a lot of stair climbing. They never did find an empty room with two beds but eventually located one that had three. We knew when we were ahead and accepted it.

There were no computers at the hotel desk. The girl used a long ruler to guide herself across a page of foolscap which contained all her reservation information. By some secret process, she determined which rooms might be empty and which might not. The interesting point was that, after the bellhop came down from checking each room, she never made any notes listing what beds the room contained. She was going to go through the same procedure again with the next guest!

In PNG, there is a rule that the Nationals MUST run the companies and be given all the jobs. They have only had since 1975 to educate their people on the complex job of running a country (and a hotel), previously administered by Australians. *In many instances, the Nationals are not yet ready to do that work.*

The hotel restaurant appeared to be an exception. The tables were all covered with tablecloths, and there were cloth napkins artistically folded into wineglasses at each place setting. The food was good and so was the service. There was one striking difference, however, from our first class hotels at home. All the neatly dressed waitresses were in bare feet!

Later that evening, in my room, I wrote my weekly article on our adventure and called the desk to place a telephone call to the newspaper back home. By this time, there was a young man in charge of the desk. He assured me he would place the call as soon as possible and notify me, in my room, when the connection was made. I called him every fifteen minutes for the next hour and was assured he was working on it. Finally, a few minutes after midnight, I returned to the desk to find another young lady in charge.

She accomplished the task for me easily. The previous clerk had gone home at the end of his shift without completing the call or passing on my request to his replacement. I wondered if perhaps he didn't know how to do it. *Possibly the only solution he could think of, was to ignore the problem – and hope that it would go away.*

In the morning, following our barefooted breakfast at the hotel, Stuart picked us up and took us back to the airport. I looked after the aeroplane while Jim flight planned for our destination, the highland bush village of Goroka. We were excited about visiting the Aboriginal natives. We wanted to learn more about their customs and their fascination with the Bird of Paradise. It has been made PNG's national bird because it is believed to carry the spirits of departed relatives.

We started up the engines, ran through our checks, taxied to the edge of the tarmac and requested our takeoff clearance. IT WAS DENIED! Apparently that phone call I had never managed to complete the night before, was more important than I had thought. The tower confirmed this to us, and we returned to the aero club to try the number again. This time I got an answer. I was told that the previous day we had entered PNG airspace without notifying them, and that I must now have clearance from their head man before we would be permitted to take off. When I asked to speak to him, I was told that he had gone to the beach for the day, and that no one else in the country could authorize our departure.

The Aero Club members were furious but explained that is the way their life has been since the Nationals took over rule in 1975. They also knew, however, that all major airspace decisions for the country are first made in a back room, by an experienced expatriot. We called this silent sentinel and I told him my story. He agreed that I could not have done more to advise them of my arrival and that he would arrange for our release. There was one problem however. The actual release had to come from the lips of the man at the beach, when he returned. So here we were – grounded for the day.

The members of the Aero Club couldn't do enough for us that day. Luckily, it was a holiday and Stuart was free to show us the sights around Port Moresby and steep us in native folklore. He was a land surveyor by profession. He explained that he had to take Nationals into his company and train them in his trade. As soon as they are able to do the work, as well as he can, Stuart will be asked to leave. Fortunately, his business is fairly complicated.

Stuart explained that there is no longer any head–hunting or · cannibalism taking place in the remote mountain villages. Since the Australians left, however, there still are tribal fights up in the hills. The practice of "Payback" is also still rampant throughout the country. Payback started as a method of getting even with an adjacent tribe for the theft of some goods or an animal. When the people gradually began drifting into the cities as squatters, they brought the practice with them. Now it exists everywhere. I read, that if you should accidentally kill a chicken or a pig with your car, you had better repay what they ask. If you don't, they consider it their absolute duty to get even with you for this offence. The fact that it was an accident is of no consequence.

Stuart also told us, that if a resident or foreigner should be unlucky enough to kill a child, who runs out in front of his car unexpectedly, that driver had better leave the country immediately. There might be enough time to sell some belongings to pay for the air fare, but not much more. *That unfortunate driver would surely be killed, as retribution, in a very short period of time. This had apparently been proven time and time again. Jim and I never drove while we were in PNG!*

During the afternoon we kept checking with the airport for word of a flight plan from our companions, Tal and Ken, indicating they would be re–joining us here as agreed before parting. When they hadn't shown up by dark we knew they would not be coming. Jim and I decided we would proceed to Darwin, Australia, in the morning as planned. If we were unable to meet with them again, this would have to become a single–plane flight the rest of the way around the world.

Before going to bed, I called the National who controlled our takeoff clearance. He was back from the beach and complained that we had never made prior application to enter his country with our plane. I pointed out to him that the International Flight Manual specifically said that prior permission was NOT required for PNG. All that was necessary was to notify them in the air en route and we had done that to the best of our ability. *He said that he had felt a need to ASSERT himself in his new position and had changed all those printed rules without notifying anyone outside of his own country.* When I asked him how someone from North America was supposed to find out about the revisions he answered, *"Well YOU know now, don't you?"* He told me he would now advise the tower to give me takeoff clearance.

In the morning a number of the South Pacific Aero Club members were there to see us off. They gave each of us a set of their club wings, which we wear proudly on our flight suits to this day. We were off the ground shortly after eight AM, and headed out over the water again, on a five and a half hour flight to the south-ernmost country on our route, Australia.

DARWIN, AUSTRALIA

When we were about 150 miles from Darwin, I called in my position report and notified them of our proposed arrival time. Suddenly, I heard Tal's voice on the air advising the same thing. I

Cape York Peninsula — The Top of Australia.

couldn't believe my ears! Tal and Ken had decided to take a short cut to Australia via Guadalcanal, in the Solomon Islands and Cairns, on the West coast of Australia. *He landed in Darwin five minutes behind us by pure coincidence.*

Before we could reunite with Tal and Ken, we had to clear customs and immigration. First we were asked to spray our cabin with a disinfectant, and then we had to pour out all the drinking water we had with us. They didn't want any foreign bacteria entering their country.

Narcotics inspection at Darwin, Australia.

After the customs and immigration officials were finished, a third uniformed man approached us with a big black dog on a leash. He asked politely if his dog could check our plane, and I realized this was to be a narcotics inspection. Without a spoken command, the intelligent animal methodically sniffed out the entire cabin area. On his way out of the cockpit, he sniffed a complete circle around the door panel – probably because that is a common place to hide drugs in an aeroplane. With those formalities out of the way, we were free to reunite with Tal and Ken again and trade stories about the past week. They had been cleared by customs and immigration the day before, when they had entered Australia at Cairns. They had luckily also missed all the red tape in PNG.

While fueling at the flying club, a mechanic noticed the Manitoba Golden Boy picture in the window of my plane. He explained that he was also from Winnipeg but had been in Australia for a number of years. He offered to put all four of us up for the night at his house. When we declined his generous offer, he drove us to the

Sheraton Hotel. He also offered to come out to the airport and help us the following day, Saturday, if either of us should have any trouble with our plane.

After supper, we went Wallaby watching, in a park at the edge of town. Wallabies are small kangaroos. At dusk they come out of the bush into clearings where they feed on the lush grass. We saw several, but it was too dark for good pictures. After admiring the Australian sunset over the harbor, we returned to the hotel. It was not much of a visit to such a large and interesting country, but we were behind schedule and promised ourselves that we would return one day for a longer stay – by jet.

BALI INDONESIA

''The Island of the Gods, Island of Smiles, Island of Temples and Dances, Island of Beaches.'' All of these describe beautiful Bali. Blessed with gentle ocean breezes 365 days of the year, Bali is best known as the setting for the musical ''South Pacific.''

After six hours aloft in the bright blue sky, with our companion plane beside us once again, we landed in this charming country, just two miles East of Java. There were no phone calls required here. When I stepped from the plane, instead of a reprimand, I was

Official Air Force welcome at Bali, Indonesia.

greeted with an official welcome. An Air Force officer and his Sargent shook my hand and said, "On behalf of my Commanding General, the head of all aviation in Indonesia, welcome to Bali, and good luck on your Round the World adventure. If there is anything we can do for you while you are here, please let us know." What a difference from PNG!

Then we were greeted by our handling crew. Their services are mandatory in Bali. They arranged for customs, immigration and fuel and then took us in their vehicle to a hotel of their choice. It was excellent and cost us only twenty-seven dollars per night. When we departed, they picked us up at the hotel again and guided us through the maze of paperwork at the airport in a friendly and efficient manner. Their one hundred dollar fee was included in our landing and parking charges when we left, and was well worth it.

All our baggage at the hotel was handled by women. There was another energy-saving device in each room. You cannot leave the air-conditioner or lights on in your room while you are out. To activate the electricity, you must insert your key in a slot, just inside the door. Of course, you can only do that when you are in the room, with your key.

Everything, on this Paradise Island, was economical. A three course dinner at Poppy's, one of the best restaurants in town, cost us about four dollars. Casette tapes, copied without royalties in Indonesia, ranged from $1.25 to $1.60 each. Every title appeared to be available. There must have been a dozen tape stores where you could select a basketful of tapes from the shelves, try them on a player, and then purchase only those tapes that you liked. We bought "give away" watches for the third world here at three for ten dollars. Jim bought a hand-carved blow gun of the type that was originally used for blowing small poison darts. We had more room and carrying capacity in the plane since the tank removal in Majuro, so he also bought a tall, hand-carved, ebony figure for his home, back in Boston.

The old culture of Bali is still strongly prevalent and can be seen throughout the island in its thousands of temples and rituals. Each morning and evening a fresh straw tray of vegetables, fruit and flowers is put out by every home and business place as an offering to the gods. Even the taxis place a fresh tray on their

Daily offerings to the Gods at Bali.

Orchestra for Balinese Dancers.

dashboards twice a day. Balinese dancers, dressed in their native, ornate costumes perform legendary dances daily for visitors, which number over 350,000 per year – mostly from nearby Australia.

A tour through the countryside showed me that the two most important things to the people of Bali are their Gods and their rice paddies. The former supports them morally and the latter, physically and economically. Indonesia is a country of one hundred and thirty-five million people, who are mostly Muslim. However, the two and a half million living on the island of Bali are primarily Hindu. Their mother–temple complex is located on Bali's hottest volcano, Gunung Agung. The island's largest and most important religious celebration is the Eka Dasa Rudra. It terminates on the volcano. It is as ambitious as it is colorful, aiming to restore a balance in the world between the forces of good and evil. *If it works in Bali, we should import it to North America.*

Rice is their principal export. The Balinese are industrious and labor long hours in the rice fields. Instead of coming out of the fields for lunch, they simply put up an umbrella, to protect themselves from the scorching sun, and take their rest where they work. Tourism, however, has given rise to many small industries, mainly wood carvings and Batik. Labor is cheap and salesmen are everywhere. It is impossible to resist buying something from these friendly people.

To the tourist, Bali's chief attraction lies in its beautiful long stretches of sand and warm water. We returned from our morning tour of the island and headed for the nearest beach for a swim. Jim brought along his camera and case. I had my money belt around me at all times – even at night. It had two pouches hanging from it – one on each side. In one side was my cash and the other side contained my passport, travellers cheques and credit cards. When we went to the beach we couldn't wear money belts so that innocent looking camera case also contained all our joint wealth and indentification.

Jim and I swam separately while the other guarded the bag. When Jim decided to have an oil massage from one of the many licensed practitioners wandering the beach, he lay down on her blanket with his camera case strap wrapped securely around his arm. No one was going to get away with all our money without Jim being the first to know about it!

But there was another reason for bringing that case with us to the beach. The beaches in Bali are topless. Before Jim left home, he bought a right–angle lens for his camera. With a fresh thirty six

A topless beach at Bali.

exposure roll for ammunition and his new toy in place, he went for a stroll on the beach. When he saw a desirable subject he would point his camera straight down the beach, but the mirrored lens was actually taking the picture of some unsuspecting girl sitting directly off to his side. *The film was not the only thing that was exposed!*

SINGAPORE

We loved Bali, but alas, it was time to move on. Our handling crew picked us up at the hotel and started us through the formalities at the airport. Everything was fine except for one small point. The flight office didn't have an authorization number for our takeoff. They contacted the Director General, to find out what was wrong. Thirty minutes later, he called back with our clearance and an apology. There had been a mix–up in their internal procedures, but none of it was our fault. It was nice to hear this for a change. Before we finished weaving our way through the Third World, we were going to consider this mere half–hour delay insignificant.

We flew six and a half hours at eight thousand feet, keeping Tal within sight beside us. Once again it was an uneventful flight in clear skies. I knew we were getting close to the Monsoon region but was quite willing to accept blue sky around me as long as it lasted.

Since this might be our final opportunity to read en route, we put the plane on autopilot and broke out our literature on Singapore. As we flew Northward, back across the equator, we were surprised to read that Singapore's two and a half million people live on a diamond shaped island just twenty-five miles long and twelve miles wide. It is so narrow that they have been forced to place the radio marker for the instrument approach to our destination airport in another country. It was across the river to the North, in Malasia.

Three quarters of the people in Singapore are Chinese; only two percent, Eurasian or European. For one hundred and ten years, British colonial rule had flourished here in European splendor. Then in 1942, victorious Japanese forces took over Singapore. After the war, there were several stages of self-determination until 1965 when it became an independent republic. Since then, it has never looked back. *Singapore is the world's busiest port and the clearing house for the region's wealth.* Ten million passengers pass through their international airport every year – one flight arrives or departs from there every minute. Small planes, like ours, are not even allowed at this airport.

We landed at Seletar Air Force Base and taxied over to the flying club. Imagine taking flying lessons in this tiny country! I understand that the flying club students can never fly straight and level for more than one minute at a time or they will find themselves outside their allotted practice area, and almost outside of their country. Their graduates must be very good at making coordinated turns. As arranged several months previously, the mechanics were ready to service our planes in the morning. The vice-president of the club turned out to be the manager of a first class hotel, The Phoenix, near the center of the city. He saved us the necessity of going through our "airline act" with the desk, to get the reduced room rate, and we gratefully checked into his establishment. There was one thing about our room that I had never seen before. Every room had a doorbell. Another surprise was that our second night was free. We didn't know until we checked out, that the aviation-minded manager had decided to donate our second night's stay as a gesture of goodwill towards our world flight.

The many new, tall, public housing buildings in this clean, modern city, attest to what Singapore has accomplished in recent years. On the way to our hotel, we passed the state prison. Above the entrance gate was a sign saying "Together we can accomplish even more." The taxis have a speed limit of eighty kilometers (fifty miles) per hour. Once that speed is reached, all commercial vehicles sound a musical chime continuously to remind and coax the driver back down below the speed limit. Tipping is also discouraged. Ten percent is automatically added to meal bills and distributed among all those connected with its preparation or delivery. This is done primarily to get the people to work together for the common good.

We had dinner that evening at the Raffles Hotel, one of the last remaining vestiges of British colonial rule. We visited the Writer's Bar, inspired by the great authors who made Raffles their second home – Noel Coward, Rudyard Kipling, Joseph Conrad and Somerset Maugham who wrote "The Moon and Sixpence" in his suite overlooking the Palm Court. Our dinner in the shaded courtyard was preceded by a Singapore Sling. This famous drink was originally created in 1915 by barman Ngiam Tong Boon in the hotel's Long Bar.

Most of the next day was spent at the flying club, watching the mechanics clean the spark plugs and change the oil and filters. While they worked, we re-organized our charts and reviewed our plans for the flights ahead. I sent Telex messages to Malasia, Thailand and Burma, advising them of our delayed arrival dates. *Both aircraft were certified by the flying club's chief engineer and signed out for the next fifty hours – through Southeast Asia and the remaining third world!*

13

The Ultimate Challenge

THAILAND AND BURMA

We were now sixteen days distant from Oakland, yet we were still able to have an early morning breakfast in Denny's. We could also have chosen Burger King or McDonalds, Singapore style. They were all within a block of each other. As I had anticipated, we were through with formation flying for awhile. The monsoons were ahead, so we flew on separate flight plans, one thousand feet apart in elevation. A non–instrument pilot could wait in this area most of the summer before waking up to a sunny forecast along his entire route.

As we flew in the cloud, we kept one radio tuned to the other plane and crossed–checked positions periodically. In five hours and twenty minutes we were in Bangkok, Thailand. The airport was divided, with one side for civilian traffic and the other for the Air Force. *Most of the supplies for Viet Nam had been dispatched some years before from the long military runway.* We landed on the civilian side and began attempting to fit our square peg into their round hole. We were the only two general aviation aeroplanes on the airport. To add to the confusion, they had an old terminal building but were also building a new one. Part of the services we required were in each terminal. There was so much construction material around that the ground controller had difficulty finding us a place to park. He finally left us out on the end of a taxi strip.

The larger aircraft using this airport all employ the services of a local handling agent. It was expensive, so once again, we did our own paper work. It took nearly five hours but, in that time, we also completed all the administration required for entry and preliminary flight planning for our departure, two days hence. We checked into the Indra Regent Hotel and were pleased to find a reply to the telex we had sent the night before to Burma, revising our arrival date there. Permission for the change was granted.

While the rest of us had been moving about the airport buildings performing our administrative duties, Ken had been guarding the luggage and making sightseeing arrangements. When we returned, he had selected one of the local tour companies. We cautioned the tour agent that we wanted a guide who spoke good English. We further specified that we wished to try out our guide that very evening, before we committed ourselves to using him again in the morning. Our schedule allowed us only one full day in this colorful country, and there were many things to see. *When we arrived at our hotel –* **SHE** *was waiting for us.*

Kay was a university graduate student who supported her parents and herself by guiding. She wore horn–rimmed glasses, was well–educated, knowledgeable and spoke excellent English. For dinner she took us to "Tumpnakthai," advertised as the world's largest and most glamorous garden restaurant. It was on 10 acres of land and consisted of 70 individual shelters, seating over 3000 guests. The shelters were separated from each other and the restaurant stage by water and a series of narrow bridges. It was delightful, as were the Thai classical dances presented during the meal.

I couldn't buy only one drink at dinner in Bangkok. When I ordered my first, I was glad that it was something I liked, for I had just bought the entire bottle. It took me a while to figure this out. At first, I thought it was novel that my waitress refilled my drink every time it came close to being empty. When my bottomless glass kept re–filling itself, I had to ask Kay what was going on before I became intoxicated and fell out of my chair into the water. Despite her conservative appearance, Kay was no prude. After dinner, our evening tour consisted of seeing the bright lights of Bangkok and then visiting one show after another. I am not entirely certain that a father and son should have been going to some of those places together. However, Kay received our stamp of approval for the following morning!

The flight from Singapore to Bangkok, for the most part, had been made in cloud and on instruments. Half a dozen thunderstorms were flashing on my stormscope, which identifies these storms by measuring the electrical discharges within the clouds. This had worried me, but it had resulted in not much more than some good aeroplane washes. I asked Kay if this was typical monsoon weather. She replied that, although this was the monsoon season, for some strange reason, the last few weeks had been fairly dry and had not produced the usual amount of rainfall. I began to hope this this pattern would continue, because the monsoons had been one of my greatest worries in planning this flight.

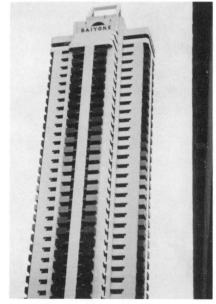

The Old and New in Bangkok.

We met Kay at 7:00 A.M. and commenced our day–long tour, which, fate was to decree, would last until well after dark. She came for the four of us in an air–conditioned micro–bus, complete with driver, cokes and ice. In the early 1970s, Bangkok had fewer than 25 buildings more than six stories high. By 1985, it had 120 high rise apartments, condominiums, office complexes and hotels. These new buildings are interspersed with the old, and harmonize with neither Thai culture nor the tropical environment. The capital of old Siam is beginning to look more like Tokyo and Hong Kong. It has also been documented to be sinking each year.

First we went down to the Chao Phraya River that runs through the heart of the city. Our river ride was in a long boat, much like Roger Moore used in the 007 movie filmed here, ''The Man With The Golden Gun.'' We passed the Oriental Hotel, reputed to be the finest in the world. There are seven staff members for every guest registered in that luxurious establishment.

Oriental Hotel — Bangkok.

A Local Laundry in a ''Klong''.

From the mainstream, we turned into one of the klongs or canals that make Bangkok the Venice of the Orient. Hundreds of thousands of people live along these klongs. They also contained hundreds of floating houseboats, until the tourist traffic in the long boats passing all day long created too many waves. The residents bathe and do their laundry in the water. They drink rain water collected from their eaves in concrete urns. The young girls bathe early in the morning, before the tourist boats arrive, but the adults

A Morning Hair Wash in Muddy Water.

don't worry about being seen by tourists. They go about their daily routine as the boats incessantly file past their doorstep. Fruits and vegetables are sold to the residents from small boats, travelling from door to door. The prices in these floating markets are about half of the price charged elsewhere, because there is no middleman, or maybe that should be "midshipman."

No visit to Bangkok is complete without seeing the Grand Palace. The palace complex contains the royal residences and the Chapel Royal of the Emerald Buddha, an object of national veneration. We sat at the feet of this one–piece jade Buddha. Crowds come to pay respect to the memory of Buddha and his teachings on the days of the week when it is open to the public. No cameras or

The Floating Market.

Ornate Construction at the Grand Palace.

shoes are allowed inside the chapel, and the bottoms of ones feet are never to face Buddha.

Our final stop within the city was at the Marble Temple. With the exception of the roof structure, the entire temple is made of

The Marble Temple, Bangkok.

Carrara marble imported from Italy. Inside are over fifty ancient, different-shaped Buddhas, which have been collected from villages all over the country and enshrined in the temple as a form of Buddhist museum.

The Bridge Over the River Kwai.

That afternoon we drove to the Burmese border, 110 miles away. The village of Kanchanaburi was the site for the construction of *The Bridge Over The River Kwai.* The bridge is not at all as it was shown in the motion picture. It is made of metal and not of wood. The bridge was not dynamited by ground forces; its two center sections were taken out in an aerial bombing raid. *The story of death in this place is, however sadly, only too true.* A museum, depicting the story, has been named the JEATH museum. This is an abbreviation for the names of the six countries involved, Japan(J), England(E), America, Australia(A), Thailand(T), and Holland(H).

Kanchanaburi Graveyard of Military Prisoners.

The Death Railway (and Bridge), as it came to be called, formed a strategic link between Thailand and Burma. It is 164 miles long in Thailand and 95 miles long in Burma. The Japanese engineers first said it would take at least 5 years to finish, but their army forced military prisoners and Thai laborers to complete it in only sixteen months. *During that short period, more than 16,000 prisoners and nearly 100,000 impressed laborers perished. They died mainly of disease, due to starvation, and a total lack of medical care. The graves of over 10,000 soldiers from the JEATH countries are there, row upon row, to remind future generations of that infamous period of history.*

While returning to Bangkok, our bus broke down. When our driver opened the hood and found the problem, I thought I was back in Oakland. The fuel pump had broken off! There was no way to repair it, and it was now getting dark. Our driver set off down the road to arrange for another van. Our breakdown had occurred right beside a roadside tire repair shop. This shop resembled a small two-bay service station, with no doors. An entire family was sitting outside in the warm night air. They welcomed us into their family group even though only Kay could talk to them. There were at least three generations living in that small building. (That must be how they fit forty-eight million people into this country, which is just three-quarters the size of Texas). Our hosts had virtually no creature comforts as we know them. Nevertheless, they had some rice on their stove and offered us a bowl, using sign language and a big friendly smile to demonstrate their hospitality. We spent several hours with these friendly people until another van could be sent from Bangkok.

As we finally neared our hotel that night, it started to rain. It was a heavy rain, and I felt certain this was a sign that the Monsoons were about to commence in earnest. I secretly hoped the rains would hold back another week until we had woven our way through the Third World.

BURMA

Bangkok is a great airport to fly out of, if you are a passenger on an airline. Their systems are definitely not geared to handle small, private planes. It took us several hours to leave – and only part of it was our fault. When I went through our approach plates to get out the ones we would be needing for Rangoon, I discovered that they weren't in our book. Once again, the military sets that we had found to be cheapest, included only airports that the American Military flies into. Luckily, Jim eventually found the offices of KLM, the friendly Dutch Airline, in the terminal. They kindly provided us with photocopies of their approach plates for Rangoon, Dacca and Kathmandu, all of which were missing from our economy sets. This is a definite note of caution for world fliers who choose the military approach plates!

After all of our bills were paid, we tried unsuccessfully to get out through many different gates to our plane. Their security is strict. Everyone knows his job. It is to NOT let you out through his gate! We eventually found a special passage, where all airline crews must pass, and were taken in a half–ton truck to our planes. Once again we had been made to feel like salmon swimming upstream.

We flew on instruments, in and out of cloud, for two and a half hours to Rangoon, Burma. It was our shortest flight to date. We flew at ten thousand feet over the mountain range between the two countries. The area below us, the intersection of Burma, Laos and Thailand, is known as the Golden Triangle. This region is the domain of the drug lords and their private mercenaries. The armies and police from the three countries stay out of it – for their health. *If we were to remain healthy too – then this was no place for us to develop engine trouble!* We didn't read anything on this flight. We just listened intently to the sweet sound of our two little smooth running engines.

As we approached Rangoon, the tower controller repeatedly asked us how many DME (distance measuring equipment) miles away we were. Usually, I can receive a signal eighty or ninety miles out but we were well inside that, and I still had no reading. The controller then checked with some other aircraft and they could not get a reading either. Suddenly our instrument came alive when we were just eighteen miles from the airport. I think they had forgotten to turn on their transmitter!

I knew there was no gas available in Rangoon, but this didn't stop their ground controller from directing us to a parking spot in their refueling area. I got out and asked the attendant if there had possibly been some change and that gas might now be available. He said ''No,'' and we moved our aeroplane to the regular parking area at the edge of their ramp. *A soldier was immediately placed on guard and we were advised to remove our overnight luggage from the plane.* As soon as our luggage was out, the customs official placed a government seal across the door. There was no inspection of the plane for drugs or other contraband. If we had any it would remain in the plane while we were visiting and depart with us when we left.

The airport at Rangoon is small, and it was easy to find our way around. The terminal building contained more employees than passengers though, and each worker seemed to need a piece of paper from us. I started to fill out one of the customary general declaration forms when the immigration official requested five

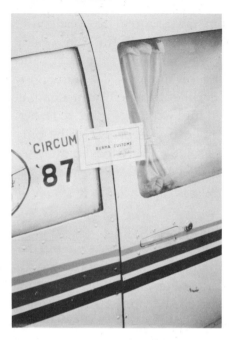

Our Aircraft Door Sealed at Rangoon.

copies. I showed him how few copies I had left on my pad and they produced a box of plain sheets and carbon paper. When I handed over my original and four carbons, I was waved on to the customs inspector. He too demanded five copies. He also advised that, although still cameras are permitted in Burma, Video cameras are not. If I had had one with me, they would have stored it in the terminal for safekeeping until our departure. My final clearance was from the chief of police. *He first required proof that I had exchanged $100.00 U.S. into local currency at the government established rate of six Kyats to the dollar.* This I did at the government booth located there for that purpose, and returned with my proof to pick up my passport and luggage. The chief politely requested five more copies of our form, found out where we were staying, advised us of the seven day maximum visit rule and cleared us into the country. I had made fifteen copies of the general declaration form and so had Tal for the other plane. As we drove away from the airport, I noticed that one copy from each set had been given to the soldier guarding our planes. Since they were written in English, I am sure he couldn't read them.

In the airport parking lot we climbed into a taxi and headed for our hotel. I was in the front seat with the driver. We had travelled only a few blocks before we pulled up and stopped beside a young man standing at the side of the road. He opened the door beside me, and with a greeting to the driver in Burmese, climbed in and shut the door. All was quiet for several minutes. Then our new travelling companion inquired, in excellent English, if we had all the local money we required. I asked him why he wished to know. He replied that in the privacy of this cab was probably the only place where we would safely be able to buy all the local money we would need for our stay, at thirty-five Kyats to the dollar. *This was approximately one-sixth of the official price we had just been forced to pay at the airport.*

I had read that the illegal exchange of foreign currency contravenes the Foreign Exchange Control Regulations in Burma. These regulations stipulate a fine and imprisonment of three years for currency violations. But I couldn't see any microphones in this dilapitated taxi, and the bills he offered did not look like the ink was still wet! We took a chance and bought enough money at this reduced rate to last us for our entire stay in Burma. I can state this since I don't expect many Burmese to read this book. The airport authorities had also given us a special form, on which we were supposed to have all our purchases and money transactions officially recorded. No one seemed to pay much attention to this form, however, once you were outside of the airport terminal or your hotel.

When we had successfully checked into our rooms and cleaned up, we took a look around our new quarters. Our hotel had originally been a British boating club during British colonial rule of Burma. During the last forty years since Burma had received its independence, the building had been put to a number of uses, including a museum. Now it was a government-run hotel and the training site for all hotel management students in Burma. It was centrally situated beside a small, but picturesque lake.

From our hotel balcony we could see, across the lake, a magnificent concrete catamaran "building." The two large concrete pontoons were tipped with large God-like figures. This was unlike anything we had ever seen. I had to rub my eyes to make certain of what I was seeing. It just didn't look like it could be real, sitting peacefully on top of the water outlined in the mist. We later learned that it was the Burmese cultural center. It is called Karaweik Hall

Karaweik Hall in Rangoon.

and seats a thousand people. One half is a dining area and the other side is a theater for cultural stage presentations. The building is actually only 15 years old, despite appearing to be an ancient treasure. It was constructed after the Osaka exposition in Japan, where a smaller replica had met with much praise. The catamaran shape represents the kind of boat that the ancient Burmese kings used for their ocean voyages.

In the city center, we visited their tourist office and arranged for a guide for the morning. It was raining, and as we pulled up in front of the Visitors Bureau, the rain increased to a deluge! I noted that it was about 2 PM. We had been told that the Monsoons were usually at their worst in the afternoons and what we were experiencing seemed to confirm it. I made a resolution to keep our flying to the mornings, if at all possible, through this part of the world.

It was raining too hard to make a run for it, so we stayed in the taxi for a few minutes and watched the locals scurry for shelter. Soon the street gutters were full of water and a number of rats came up out of the sewer system for air. Everything below ground was now full of water so the rats ran across the sidewalk, amongst the running pedestrians, into a nearby building.

Inside the tourist bureau (the SOLE tour operator and travel agent for Burma) we bought tickets for dinner and the cultural show that evening at Karaweik Hall. Unfortunately, there was no possibility of us visiting Pagan. That Birthplace of Burmese culture contains over 5000 sacred pagodas but it is located 310 miles North of Rangoon. There were no commercial flights scheduled, and private planes are strictly prohibited from flying there. We would therefore have to find out about Burma in Rangoon. So we made our usual request for a good English speaking guide for the following morning. Then we returned to our hotel to prepare for our night out on that concrete catamaran across the lake.

Dinner at Karaweik Hall was authentic, but not something for which we would want the recipe. However, the classical dancing show was excellent. Some of the dances were pure dance and some were dance drama, depicting the life of Buddha. I noticed that all the female dancers wore dresses with white cloth about the bottom of the skirt – trailing like a mini train. Each time they changed direction, they first had to kick this train into the air and make their turn while it was airborne. It was beautifully done! I am sure that what we saw represented many years of practice. One of the performances, the Chin–lone or the Cane Ball dance, was completely different. Real Cane Ball is played by five or six Burmese men standing in a circle. The cane ball is bounced around the circle without touching the ground. This is accomplished by kicking with the toes, heels or knees. Our performance was capably given by a young lady alone on stage. I suspect there are many teams of men in the country that would welcome her into their circle – perhaps even as their captain.

The policy of isolation in Burma has caused the country to lag significantly behind the rest of the world. They don't appear to have obtained a new bus or truck since the British went home, over 40 years before. Most of the men in Rangoon wore a sarong type of skirt. When accompanying tourists, some guides wore long pants, but that does not appear to be the norm. We had a telephone in our room but the directory was a year old. About two–thirds of the numbers were government officials or bureaus. I got the feeling that the ordinary citizen, living in his modest hut, doesn't have five or six telephones around the house like we have come to expect in North America.

I tried to phone ahead from Burma to revise our arrival times in the next two countries, but the phone calls wouldn't go through.

I went down to the central hotel switchboard and I could see why. The switchboard was the type where the operator pulls a cord, with a plug on its end, up from her console and pushes it into a hole, on the panel in front of her, to make the connection and extinguish a signal light. It must have been at least fifty years old. Very early in the morning on the day we were leaving Burma, I was finally able to get some calls through to other countries. I called home and the newspaper to which I was reporting weekly. I also tried again, without success, to revise my arrival date at Dacca, our next stop. I paid for the two completed calls with my black market Kyats, which made these calls among the cheapest on the trip.

The Shwedagon Pagoda in Rangoon.

We did end up with an excellent guide. His name was Sidney, and he met us in the morning with one of the very few air-conditioned cars in Rangoon. He commenced our three hour tour with a visit to the Shwedagon Pagoda, near the center of town. Often referred to as the Golden Pagoda, it is said to contain more gold on its surface than Fort Knox. More important though, it is also reputed to contain several hairs of Buddha. These sacred hairs are said to be located within the original pagoda which is now encased in this larger one. The Pagoda is solid, over 200 feet high without rooms or chambers inside. To confirm the existence of those sacred hairs of Buddha would be a formidable task!

Spaced evenly among the shrines encircling the pagoda, are seven altars representing each day of the week. The average North American doesn't know, or particularly care, on which day of the week he or she was born. The Burmese do! They go regularly to their birthday shrine, pay a few Kyats, and pour holy water over the God–like statue representing their day of the week. This is supposed to bring them luck and happiness for the following seven days. Saturday was the busiest shrine because it is supposed to be the Satan's day, and those Burmese born on Saturday require extra protection if they are to survive the week.

We had lunch at the Strand Hotel and learned a little about our tour guide. Sidney is an entrepreneur. He sells things, repairs cars, and helps arrange connections for people both in and out of the country. The Burmese people are not allowed to leave their country unless they have a letter from a host in another country guaranteeing their passage, lodging, and all their spending money while they are away. They are not permitted to take any Kyats out of the country. Sidney has made several trips to the United States. He said that he has foreign friends take money out for him and place it in a Thai bank account for him. He also acts as an agent for several foreign importers, who made their first contacts in Burma while he was acting as their tour guide.

Sidney said he is also going to write a book on tourism in Burma, an industry which will now be severely depressed in light of the recent political instability. The black market is rampant there and, in fact, is a vital part of the economy. Because of this, there are many tourists who arrive with only a backpack and a couple of bottles of whiskey to trade. They contribute little or nothing to the economy. Sidney wants to write about the other kind – the ones he has guided over the years. These are the visitors who bring with them real American dollars and spend them in the country the way a tourist should. We were his first round–the–world tourists, so we should find a place in his book – if he ever writes it.

Around town, we passed medical clinics that didn't appear clean enough to enter, let alone to be the place in which to receive medical attention. Sidney explained that the whole country operates in a corrupt socialistic system. Everybody is on the ''take.'' There is a pretense of running a socialized system but everyone knows it's artificial. The doctors practice socialized medicine in these run-down clinics only until mid-afternoon. They then go to their private offices and practice private modern medicine, attending to the politicians and the fortunate few who can afford to pay them on the side.

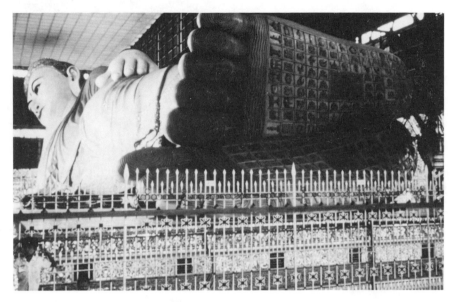

The Reclining Buddha at Chauk Htat Gyi Monastery, Burma.

Sidney then drove us to see the Reclining Buddha. This gargantuan statue measures 230 feet long. It rests under a partially open enclosure built to protect it, that is large enough to house a modern jumbo jet aircraft. The reclining Buddha is located within the compound of the Chauk Htat Gyi monastery complex and draws a regular stream of worshippers. On both its feet are inscribed nine rows of ancient symbols telling the story of Buddha. The sheer size of this Buddha is really very impressive.

We asked Sidney to take us to the local market area. Perhaps we shouldn't have! We parked several blocks away and walked through town. We were immediately followed by a woman carrying a baby with scabs all over its head. The woman looked about twenty-two years old but she had no teeth. She was crying and pleading with us for help. It was virtually impossible to discourage her since her problem was simple – it was survival! People squatted all over the street selling their pitifully meagre wares. One lady had six flashlight batteries for sale. Another sat with a box of wooden rulers in front of her. We didn't stay there very long. It was too depressing. One thing we saw, however, is worth relating.

Selling Snake Feces in the Public Market, Rangoon.

Squatting on a plastic sheet in the market area was a young man with a basket full of snakes. In front of him were piles of dried snake feces he had previously collected. He was selling this product as a generalized medical cure. Sidney said that he was even recommending that it be rubbed on open wounds. A number of locals bought some as I gazed in amazement. I couldn't believe it! If I ever invent an unusual product and have trouble marketing it, I think I will send for that young Burmese salesman.

14

The Ultimate Challenge

BANGLADESH AND NEPAL

It was our twenty–first day since leaving Oakland when we woke up in Rangoon for the last time and took one of their open taxi–trucks to the airport. Of course, it broke down! After all our previous troubles, I naturally suggested that the trouble was more than likely a broken fuel pump, but our driver and his assistant seemed to know exactly what to do. They removed the sump from the gas line and drained out the Monsoon rain water that somehow finds its way into the gas supply in Burma. The engine spluttered, but it eventually ran and we got to the airport after about a half–hour delay.

There, we found that the necessary clearance to go to Dacca in Bangladesh had still not come through. Without this permission, we would not be allowed to leave Burma. All of our previous telephone efforts had apparently proved unsuccessful. I showed everyone the letters of preliminary approval that I had received several months prior, and we were taken to the flight control center – their equivalent of our radar control room. The chief explained that they do not have telephone communication with Dacca. If he couldn't phone them from this airport control center, it was no wonder I couldn't do it from the hotel!

They seated me at one of their control desks and presented me with a pair of earphones and a microphone. They explained that this was a High Frequency radio, like the one I had used in my plane for long range communication over the ocean. If I could find someone on the other end of this radio to say it was O.K. to come to Dacca, we would be permitted to leave Burma. Through the static, I managed to make contact with the Dacca control center. I explained to my listener about our original authority to come to Dacca, and the mechanical problems that had delayed us, changing our arrival date. I was told that they would look into it, and for the next fifteen minutes we sat around the control center waiting for an answer. We smiled at the controllers and they smiled back. Everyone assured everyone else that this was all going to work out fine, but we remained very tense. If the answer was "No," what would we do next? We had no wish to take out citizenship in Rangoon, Burma!

Finally, my earphones started to crackle and, over the static, I picked out the words for which I was waiting. Our flight was approved! I then realized that I was the only one who could hear this wonderful news. I asked the officials in the room if this receiver could be connected to a loudspeaker for all to hear. A switch was thrown and I requested my distant friend to repeat the magic words. He again said "Permission is granted!" The whole room became animated, for they were all on our side, really anxious to help. Immediately, the wheels went into motion, the remaining paperwork resolved itself quickly, and we were on our way.

I suggested that Tal and Ken might like to go first, as we had been the lead plane since we rejoined each other again in Darwin. Both crews planned for the minimum en route altitude of 12,000 feet. We couldn't fly lower because of the terrain and didn't want to go higher because we would need supplemental oxygen. Tal took off, and following the mandatory fifteen minute separation, Jim and I followed him into the clouds. It was to be a short flight, just three and a half hours. We were in and out of cloud and rain showers, and I was pleased that we had received our authority in time to complete our flight in the morning, before the Monsoon rains became heavy in the mid-afternoon.

Suddenly, Tal burst on the inter–aircraft radio frequency. Excitedly, he shouted that he was being intercepted by two jet fighters! He exclaimed that the fighters had broken out of a cloud and shot right in front of his plane, left to right! They had missed him by mere feet! The fighters were now returning and coming up alongside him, one on each side. After they had a good look at his aircraft, they disappeared into the cloud and were not seen again.

Later, we reconstructed the events and came to the following conclusions. We had been advised to report to Dacca control, when we crossed the Bangladesh border, and Tal was in the process of doing this when the near–miss occurred. Dacca was still some distance away, but immediately under our flight path, just inside the Bangladesh border, was the city of Chittagong, an air force base for Bangladesh. Burma was not used to vectoring low–level flights into Dacca and forgot about this military zone. The two jet fighters had taken off from Chittagong on a practice exercise and were unaware of our presence in their skies. They were just as surprised as Tal had been, and both parties reported the near–miss when they landed. I couldn't help but reflect on some of the circumstances that placed Tal in that particular air space at that exact time. First, there was the water in our taxi's fuel on the way to the airport. Then there was the delay in getting permission to take off. Finally, there was my suggestion that Tal might like to go first for a change. If any one of these events had not occurred, that frightening encounter would not have taken place.

Our reception in Dacca was most cordial. The customs official asked us for only one general declaration form. We had just used fifteen copies per aeroplane to clear Burma, yet here we could enter with only **one**. *It was difficult for me to understand why there was so little co–ordination between two countries sharing a common border.*

I had written ahead to arrange for fuel in Dacca. As we came to a stop on the tarmac, the drums of fuel started rolling out toward our aeroplanes. There had not been a propellor plane, that used avgas, on this airport for over two years. All flying in planes like ours is done from a small airport some distance away. There, the flying club has pumps for transferring the gas from the drums into the planes. There were, however, no such facilities on this international airport. Although obtaining a pump was next to impossible, finding many able and willing hands was simple. Nearly every-

"Human Hand Valve", Dacca.

thing is done by hand in Bangladesh. The fuel manager soon rounded up seven helpers, some pails, funnels and a chamois for filtering the fuel. There was no valve or tap for the drums, so one of the employees was appointed to be the "human hand valve" and the "chain gang gas delivery" commenced. I made certain no one lit a match in the vicinity of this makeshift operation, because fuel was being spilled from the pails at both ends of the operation. Tal and I each took two full drums, or perhaps I should say that we each paid for that quantity. The amount that actually arrived inside the plane's fuel tanks was somewhat less. To my surprise, when this unorthodox procedure was all finished, I was able to pay for the performance with a Shell credit card.

Next, we went over to their flight planning office. Everyone there already knew all about us, because of the near–miss report. Calculating our fees was more difficult than getting the fuel. Their rate sheets didn't go down far enough to accommodate our small planes so they had to extrapolate. They finally decided on $4.00 for landing, $2.00 for using their communication system and $1.00 for parking. To this $7.00 total they had to add their minimum security fee of $100.00. This was their charge for having a soldier guard the aeroplanes, and they apologetically explained that it was the absolute minimum they were allowed to charge any aircraft on that field. They also insisted we pay with American dollars. We really had no complaint. Everyone had gone out of their way to accommodate us. Their airport actually had handled us with less fuss than either Bangkok or Rangoon.

We were not expecting to find a good hotel in this impoverished country, so were surprised to discover we had the choice of at least two luxury hotels. An agent at the airport offered us air-crew rates (half-price) and free transportation to his five star hotel, the Sonergon. We readily accepted and while checking in, were advised that the manager was a Canadian and would probably like to meet us. His name was Jan Segars and he entertained us royally. We met for cocktails and he treated the four of us to dinner in the hotel dining room.

Jan explained that his hotel is like an oasis in Dacca. Despite abject poverty on all sides, everything inside his hotel was first class. For example, our beds had sheets, both above and below the blankets, so that our chins would never have to touch anything unlaundered. While we were at dinner, the towels that we had used, were exchanged for fresh ones and, of course, chocolates were placed on our made-down beds. I had difficulty convincing myself that I was in one of the poorest countries in the world! I asked Jan who would use such a luxury hotel and why it was here. He explained that it was primarily used by two groups. The first were foreign buyers for the textile industry. The other consisted of politicians and staff from around the world who come here to supervise the allocation of aid from their respective countries. They come to help the underprivileged but are not interested in suffering along with them.

The hotel was surrounded by a high fence and armed guards. Outside, poverty and destitution stretched in all directions. The people were lucky to have a sheet of canvas to suspend between two poles to call home. We decided that there was nothing new to be seen that we hadn't already just experienced in neighboring Burma. We waived our sightseeing day and opted to continue on in the morning, gaining back one more lost day from our schedule.

Jan met us again in the morning for breakfast and arranged for two air-conditioned Mercedes cars to escort us to the airport in convoy. He accompanied us and his airport staff facilitated our departure. This was of considerable help, and we were grateful for all the assistance our fellow-Canadian had provided.

NEPAL

Jim and I took the lead, since Tal and Ken still had their "near miss" fresh in their memory. We climbed through the cloud to 12,000 feet and found ourselves in clear, blue sky. It was still an instrument flight however, so Tal was required to stay separated well behind us. Three hours later, we approached the Kathmandu control area and established radio contact. They requested our entry number, but we didn't have one. I explained about our preliminary permission and my later revisions to our arrival date. They didn't seem to have a record of any of these communications, even when I read them my original letter and gave them its file number. Despite being in cloud and on a direct course for the Himalaya mountains, they were hesitant to allow us in their control area. Finally, after Jim insisted, they grudgingly accepted and allowed us into their air space.

We were cleared for a long VOR DME approach and started back down through the thick layer of forboding cloud and Monsoon rain, which had been just below us throughout the flight. Kathmandu is in a small valley surrounded by mountains, and the approach is through a narrow mountain gorge. The valley floor is 4,000 feet above sea level and the surrounding mountain rim is at least 3,000 feet above that. Just beyond this inner ring of rocks the actual Himalayas reached much higher. *The approach chart indicated that an aircraft was safe below 8,000 feet, only if it stayed within 4 miles of the airport.* Our approach commenced at around 12,000 feet and, for awhile, we went strictly according to the chart. I continuously called out our distance and altitude. Jim kept us on the correct approach radial and controlled the aircraft's descent to match the published numbers. I knew the ceilings below us were down to absolute minimums for IFR. The air was smooth but it was pouring rain.

Suddenly, the controller requested our present height. We were at 9,500 feet and descending. *She told us to level off there until further notice!* Someone had cleared another aeroplane for takeoff down below us, and it would not be safe for us to descend further in the cloud until that aircraft had climbed to 8,000 feet and left the valley. This was Third World controlling at its worst. We maintained our approach heading and passed over the airport completely in cloud well below the height of the mountains around us. The valley was only eight miles wide, so we decided to fly a tight circular impromptu holding pattern until we were cleared to descend further.

Eventually, after several terse exchanges, we received clearance to continue the approach. However, we couldn't return to where this approach had started, because we were now too low. We quickly designed an approach of our own. Since there is no radar at Kathmandu, they wouldn't know our flight path anyway. Jim descended in a tight circle, and we rejoined the approach radial on the VOR. Then we turned in toward the airport. The approach chart called for us to be at 5,800 feet, four miles from the runway, but we were still at 8,000. Our adrenalin was flowing now. The cloud remained thick and the Monsoon rains were unrelenting. Jim dove the plane at a steep angle down along the runway radial, and I kept calling out distance and altitude. At minimums I strained to see the runway through the pelting rain, while Jim remained fixed on the instruments. All my senses peaked together. Gradually lights became faintly visible and then at last the runway outline. *What a welcome sight! We had just successfully completed one of the toughest flying assignments of the trip. Never before had we been forced to modify an approach as it was being flown, in a foreign country, and in the middle of the highest mountain range in the world!*

The authorities were good to us. They requested only one copy of our general declaration and then even suggested that we could put both aeroplanes on the one form. When I set my watch to local time I got another surprise. Nepal makes only a fifteen minute time change. Most countries adjust their time zones one hour at a time and a few refine that to half an hour, but the Nepalese go one step further. They are a gentle people and a pleasure to meet. In many material ways they are centuries behind us, but as human beings, many of them seem light years ahead of us.

We chose the Mount Everest Sheraton Hotel. Once again, our flight suits and our Pilot's Association membership cards cut the hotel rate in half to $44.00 per day, double occupancy. Those last two words caused some confusion at the desk. When we phoned from the airport to reserve the rooms, we told them it was for four pilots so they had four keys out on the counter waiting for us when we arrived. I told the clerk that we were sharing the rooms and would only require two. He immediately commenced assigning Tal and me a room together. I explained that was wrong for I would be sharing a room with Jim. The clerk looked puzzled. *What kind of an airline was this where each of the middle-aged pilots specified a young one with whom to share his room?*

Bus Transporation, Kathmandu.

Contrary to custom, the rain let up in the afternoon, so we went sightseeing. The word "Kathmandu" means wooden house, and refers to a particular large house in the center of town which is said to have been made from a single tree.

Nepal is unique in that up until 1951, there were no visitors allowed into the country, and there were no motor vehicles there until 1956. Now, visitors and cars are everywhere. It is almost impossible to tell where you are supposed to walk and where the cars are supposed to travel. It appeared the drivers simply kept one hand on the horn and the other on the wheel, while they threaded their way through the pedestrians and cyclists. There was no electric power in Nepal until the 1960s. We were in a country that had come out of cultural isolation less than thirty years ago. The illiteracy rate is sadly still over 70% and there is no compulsory schooling. Nobody appears to have very much but they all seemed

Sacred cows lie all day undisturbed in roadway outside Sheraton Hotel.

content and happy. One thing they do have is cows, and the cows run freely throughout the city! They lie down in the center of the roads and the cars go willingly around them. These priveleges are afforded by the Hindu religion, which teaches that cows are the reincarnation of loved ones and are therefore sacred. Monkeys are also sacred and they run free in the countryside, particularly around the temples. The Sherpas of Nepal are a Mongolian race who claim to have migrated to their present home from eastern Tibet. Traditionally, the Sherpas spent their summers in Tibet and their winters in Nepal. When they discovered the potato, they began cultivating it and settled permanently in Nepal. They were also traders, importing goods from Kathmandu, Nepal, and trading it with the Tibetans. When the Dali Lama fled Tibet and the border was closed by the Chinese, they were forced to look for alternative means of support. They found this in acting as guides and bearers for trekking and climbing expeditions. Over the years, their bodies have adapted to the high altitudes of the Himalayas. They live in permanent villages as high as 14,000 feet and can function as easily at 19,000 feet as the rest of the world does at sea level.

Sherpas are devout Buddhists. They are permitted to eat some meat, but they must hire others to slaughter their livestock. One day a year, during the autumn Dasian festival, each village kills over one hundred water buffalo. This can amount to 10,000 animals throughout Nepal over this one week festival. Normally, their animals are sacrificed every Tuesday in special temples around the countryside. The citizens bring a male chicken, goat or other family animal to the temple. A worker from one of the lower Hindu castes cuts off its head and rubs its blood over effigies surrounding the killing room. A priest then blesses the remains. According to their beliefs, this has released an ''unfortunate brother'' from his imprisonment as an animal and permits him to be reborn as a man. The satisfied owner of the sacrificial animal then pays the priest a few rupees, takes his meat home and eats it. We had an opportunity to witness this fascinating ritual, but all agreed we preferred the North American approach to meat packing.

Most of the local people had a red spot in the middle of their forehead. This is called a Tika and is a sign that the person has completed his daily

Elderly Roadside Merchant, Nepal.

worship at one of the temples. It is a symbol of the presence of the divine. Early in the morning, the devout visit their temples carrying a copper dish piled with rice, red powder and tiny yellow flower petals to scatter over the image of their God. Afterward, they mix the remains of their offering with clay and place a spot of the red mixture on their foreheads, between the eyes. The Tika is washed off at night to ensure a temple visit again the following day.

Prayer Wheels

Their temples often contained rows of Prayer Wheels. These are small brass drums, pivoted top and bottom, with prayers inscribed on their outer surface. Busy worshipers spin the wheels as they walk by, thus effectively saying the prayers that are written around them . A person can get in a lot of praying this way, in a very short time.

We visited an old building in the town square where the **Living Goddess of Nepal** resides. Called the Kumari Bahal, she is selected from the Sakya clan of goldsmiths and silversmiths when she is but four or five years old. Her body must be flawless and must satisfy 32 specified, distinctive signs. The girl's courage is tested by leaving her inside this ancient structure, alone in the dark, for one whole night, after men, masked as demons, try to

Home of the Living Goddess — Kathmandu.

scare her, and bloody animal heads are placed around her in the darkness. Finally, she must correctly select some item which belonged to the previous Kumari from among a collection of similar items. If she passes these tests, she becomes the Living Goddess. She then leaves her family and moves into her new home with an appointed custodian family. Their responsibility is to look after her needs and welfare. From that moment on, her feet must never touch the ground outside her new home. She is exhibited to the public three times a year during certain festivals but is carried by bearers while she is outside of her home. When she reaches puberty, or otherwise loses blood from a wound, she must leave and give up her appointment to a successor.

Taking her picture is forbidden. Inside the house courtyard visitors are watched closely by the Princess' surrogate father. When all the photographs of the building have been taken and all cameras returned to their carrying cases, the virgin Goddess shows herself briefly at an upstairs window. She was a little girl – about 9 years old. Our guide told us that ex–princesses are not much in demand as wives because they are spoiled and have never learned to work. And in Nepal, work is the key ingredient to staying alive.

Cremation ceremony, Nepal.

One unforgettable Nepalese custom is their handling of the dead. As soon as a person dies, usually within a few hours, the male relatives assemble and take the body to cremation platforms, called ghats, beside the Bhagmati river for immediate cremation. En route, they stop and pay between $25.00 and $2500.00 for firewood and funeral oils. The oils or butters are fragranced and obviously aid in combustion. Jutting out into the river there were six ghats. Four were for public use, one for senior officials, and one for Royalty. Three public cremations were quietly in progress while we watched.

First, they build the funeral pyre from the purchased wood. The body, wrapped in a white shawl, is carried around the pyre three times and then placed upon it. The priest then walks around the body three times carrying a butter lamp, and places a wick in the deceased's mouth. The clothing is then removed discretely from under the shawl and tossed into the river. The mouth is set afire first. Our guide noted that this was so that the voice of the deceased could precede the body to the afterlife and announce the spirit's arrival. The body torso is then covered with straw and the whole pyre is ignited. When cremation is complete, the ashes are swept into the river. According to Hindu religion, all life must end in the river which flows to the Ganges.

There is no death certificate required before cremation. A certificate has to be filed by the family with the civic authorities within 45 days, simply to record that the person no longer exists. The whole system sounded very casual to me but it seems to work for them. I guess one reason it works is because no one has any rich old relatives in Nepal. I also presume that pathologists in Nepal suffer from chronic unemployment.

Children hammering rocks into gravel.

In the afternoon, we left Kathmandu and toured the countryside. Like Bangladesh, most work is performed entirely by hand. Sand trucks are driven into shallow river beds and the sand shoveled into the trucks by hand. Two men sat by the roadside with a long saw, ripping heavy timbers manually into dimension lumber. Two girls were using a hammer to break up a pile of stones into road gravel. Despite not having minimum wage laws, no one appeared unhappy.

As we wound our way along a hillside highway, we could see a community far below us beside a small river. There was only one narrow road leading to it. It was their Leper Colony.

We also drove past an army barracks with a showy Gurkha soldier in full dress on guard at its gate. These brave troops from the isolated hills of Nepal, have been famous for their fierceness and bravery in warfare since the late 18th century, and have bolstered the British and Indian armies since 1886. Most recently, they played a key role in the 1982 Falkland Islands crisis.

Overhead supply tramway.

Crossing the road ahead of us, we noticed what appeared to be a ski-lift travelling across flat country instead of up a hill. That puzzled me and we stopped to investigate. The answer was fascinating. The road from Kathmandu to India is about 40 miles long and, is so full of potholes, that trucks trying to use it have a very short life span. The cost of repairing and maintaining the road through the mountains has proved to be prohibitive so ground transportation for supplies is unreliable. Because of this, they have built this ''supply tramway.'' The tramway travels in straight lines and is therefore much shorter than the road. It can accommodate 20 tons distributed among the many little platforms suspended along its length. We watched a number of loads of cement pass above us on their way to Kathmandu, before carrying on with our journey.

We continued on to a nearby town, Bhaktapur. It is also known as the woodcarver's town. The buildings are nearly all made of wood and are adorned with hand-carved figures. Their temple is guarded by a series of animals and gods. As one climbs the stairs to the temple, each new figure encountered is reputed to be ten times as powerful as the last. The theory is that, with this kind of protection, no harm will be able to make it safely up the long entrance stairway into the temple building itself.

Jim and the "Baby Sitters", Bhaktapur, Nepal.

In the Bhaktapur town square, Jim spotted a young girl carrying her baby brother on her back. The little boy was sound asleep and Jim thought this would make a good picture. He used sign language to indicate what he wanted and, when she agreed to a picture, he handed me his camera. Before Jim could get her properly posed, another little girl decided that there was a rupee to be made, and ran into the picture. After I snapped the shutter, Jim gave each of the girls a rupee and began to walk away. There was a tug on his pantleg. The first little girl pointed over her shoulder to her little brother and held up two fingers. Two people should get two rupees – not one!

We were both impressed with this little entrepreneur and Jim quickly rewarded her with the additional rupee and tried once more to leave. Not so fast! The other little girl also wanted a second rupee. With a series of signs, Jim convinced her that she could only have one rupee because, in her case, he had only taken a picture of one person. Begrudgingly, she accepted the fact and walked away. Jim and I continued our tour of the old wooden buildings around the square. Minutes later, the second little girl was back. She was carrying a little baby girl, she had borrowed somewhere, and was proudly holding up two fingers toward us. Jim couldn't deny her any longer - she received her other rupee.

Around 2 PM the Monsoons came again. We had hoped to travel farther, to a lookout point, for a view of Mount Everest. Alas, this was the wrong season for that. The locals suggested we return in November when the skies are normally clear. That is the month when the major climbs and mountain treks take place. It was good advice, but Jim could only obtain time off for this trip in July and August.

Himalayan Peaks — Nepal.

A layer of cloud covered the entire Kathmandu basin when we departed. Our three hour flight to New Delhi, India, had to commence with a tight climbing circular departure out of this mountain–ringed valley. The flight was again on instruments. Just before we reached flight–planned altitude, we broke free of cloud into the Nepalese sunshine. To the northeast were the fabled

Himalayas, including Mount Everest. We didn't have to wait until November! Our last climbing turn was deliberately extended. It took us alongside the overwhelming Himalayan peaks. I drank in the once–in–a–lifetime view and considered my visit to Nepal complete.

The people of Kathmandu will live in our memory forever. They lead a simple life but seem happy with their lot. They have traditions that, to us, appear bizarre but are friendly, gentle and cooperative. Nepal was a very pleasant country to visit.

15

The Ultimate Challenge

INDIA AND PAKISTAN

Monsoon rains are dependably undependable. The weather cleared as we approached the Indian border. Instead of being drenched by Monsoons, India was in a drought. It was their driest Monsoon season in over one hundred years. The dearth of moisture was evident everywhere as we flew over the parched countryside. What little vegetation we could see, appeared sparse and pale brown. The sky was clear and the sun was merciless. Our approach into New Delhi airport was probably one of the easiest of the trip. We appeared to be their only customer. Things changed, however, after we landed.

The ground controller directed us to the large concrete apron alongside their modern international terminal building but wouldn't tell us where to park. *Several times we taxied toward one of their commercial aircraft unloading zones, and each time a soldier appeared with a weapon and waved us away.* When I complained about this predicament to the tower, they eventually assigned us a parking stall across the apron outside some maintenance buildings. Each numbered area was large enough to park a jumbo jet. When Tal landed a few minutes later, and parked in his assigned spot, Jim and I moved our plane over beside him.

Two aeroplanes parked in the same numbered spot was more than they could bear – even though combined, we occupied less than half of it. Out came the officials. They eventually saw the logic of our manoeuvre and finally permitted us to remain where we were. Then came the shocker! I was told that there was no avgas on this airport – only jet fuel. Once again we had landed at the international airport, because we had to obtain customs and immigration clearance. Avgas, however, was available only at domestic airports, which served the smaller Indian towns using a variety of **propellor** aeroplanes. I couldn't understand this, because our International Flight Manual listed this airport as having avgas available.

However, on the other side of this same airport, was another airport with a completely different name, its own runways and control tower. It was the domestic airport and avgas was available there. Special permission was obtained for us to taxi over for fuel and then return and clear customs and immigration at the international airport where we were presently parked. Since we were technically still "in bond," we couldn't leave our aeroplanes or enter their terminal. The temperature was unfortunately over 100 degrees!

On the other airport tarmac, we asked our new ground controller to call the fuel truck for us. I sat under the wing of our aeroplane to avoid the intense sun and waited. No one came. I called the tower again every few minutes, until I was told abruptly that the gas truck would get to us when it was ready to! About two hours later the fuel depot manager came out to interview us to make certain that our proposed method of payment was satisfactory. *I assured him I had the money and reached for my money belt to show him. I got the shock of a lifetime! The pouches on the money belt weren't there! I was certain that I had put the belt on under my flight suit before I left the hotel that morning!*

The next two minutes were among the longest of the entire trip. With my heart pounding and adrenaline racing, I desperately felt up and down both legs and checked inside the plane. The belt should not have broken, because I had the clasp double-stitched for safety at the shoemaker before I left home. There was still a substantial sum of money in the two pouches hanging from that belt **somewhere**. Gone also were my credit cards, travellers cheques and passport!. I was afraid that pernicious "Murphy" had caught up with me again! Then my hands wandered around to the small of my back. A flood of relief surged through me. There were two previously undetected lumps there! Somehow, for the first time on the trip, the money pouches had slid along the belt, around behind me. Perhaps this happened when I crawled on the asphalt under the wing to avoid the murderous sun. Anyway, my funds and documents were secure. We obtained our gas, taxied the aircraft back across to the other airport and cleared ourselves through customs and immigration, into the country.

Before we left the terminal, I asked why the entire international airport was so empty. Our group appeared to be the only non–employees in that huge structure. I was told that it is always empty during in the daytime, but that the terminal comes alive at night. Most European cities have an early evening takeoff curfew in effect for jet aircraft because of residential noise. New Delhi has no such curfew so all the European airlines, to gain maximum utilization of their fleet, schedule their aircraft to take off for India, just before their European departure curfews come into effect. These jets arrive in New Delhi all night long.

We selected the Taj Palace Hotel for our stay in New Delhi and it was excellent. Our evening meal was served in their Orient Express Car. Constructed inside the hotel, it was a replica of the dining car on that famed European train, supposedly correct in every detail. It was a very unique theme for a restaurant. The china and silver were exquisite and the food delicious. The waiters and maitre d'hotel wore white gloves. I had difficulty believing that I was in India and not in France.

Early the next morning, we began our 130 mile journey south to visit the Taj Mahal in Agra. We hired another private air-conditioned car, as the price was not much different than four fares on one of the tour buses. We had considered flying ourselves to Agra, but our administrative experiences at the airport the day before had taught us better. The one landing we had already made into that bureaucratic airport quagmire was sufficient. *It actually was a good decision to drive to Agra because the road is the country's lifeline, and provided a panorama of everyday life in India.*

I think we saw examples of nearly all of India's lifestyles on that one highway. There were thousands of people walking and thousands more riding bicycles. The road was shared equally by

Main highway to Agra, India.

cars, buses, elephants, cows and camels. We passed several over-turned trucks and damaged cars still occupying the middle of the road. Dead animals, bloated and rigoured into grotesque positions, littered the shoulders. The dense, mixed traffic just travelled unconcernedly around everything. No one appeared to be doing anything to clear the road or right the vehicles. They appeared oblivious to the carnage. Whenever we passed a water pond, it was invariably filled with water buffalo cooling themselves from the heat of the day. *To have missed witnessing this roadside montage would have been to have missed seeing India!*

Nothing is wasted in this impoverished country. Along the roadside, the water buffalo and cows deposit their excrement. The local people gather it up, shape it into circular patties and set it to dry in the sun. When it is dry, they gather and store the patties in piles shaped like small houses, much as bales of hay are sometimes stored on this continent. Later they are sold or used for fuel.

Agra is a city of one million people, and was the capital of India in the 17th century when the Taj Mahal was built. There are no factories in the city. In an attempt to provide employment for its artisans, and keep the air clean to preserve the priceless marble of the Taj Mahal, anything made by machine in Agra is subject to a 300% duty.

The Taj Mahal is located on the south bank of the Jumna river, just outside Agra. Taj Mahal means "palace for Mahal." It was built by the Mogul emperor, Shah Jahan, in memory of his beloved

The Taj Mahal, Agra, India.

wife who was called Mumtaz–i–Mahal, "chosen one of the palace." She had borne him 14 children during their 18 year marriage. Before she died during childbirth, she called the Emperor back from battle specifically to ask three things from him in return for her constant love. Firstly, he should not marry again. Secondly, he should take good care of their children. Finally, he should build her a burial place of such magnificence that it could never be built again by others.

Construction commenced in 1632, after plans had been prepared by a council of architects from India, Persia, central Asia and beyond. *More than 20,000 workmen were employed daily for 22 years to complete the complex.* The Taj is built from white Indian marble which is harder and more durable than Italian Carrera marble. Indian marble also has embedded quartz crystals, which result in the many varying shades and colors it presents in the different

Lacework Marble Panel — Taj Mahal.

lights of the day. The marble is also translucent and glows at sunset and sunrise. The masons, inlayers and calligraphists, have performed their work without equal. The joints in the pieces of marble are barely discernible. The inlaid semi–precious stones, like jade, jasmine, and green turquoise, are set into the marble in a fascinating array of decorative patterns. The interior, main floor burial crypts are encircled by a fence of intricate marble lacework panels. Each panel (roughly the size of a sheet of modern plywood) took ten men, ten years to fashion from a single slab of marble. It was a breathtaking sight!

The Mogul's son thought his father was disturbed. When the son gained enough authority to do so, he had him locked up. The father spent the rest of his years in confinement, but was given a room that overlooked the Taj where his beautiful wife was buried. On his death, the son relented and permitted his father to be buried alongside his loving wife in the center of the Taj Mahal.

Our ride back to New Delhi became interesting when the Monsoon rains came once again. Perhaps it was not a full Monsoon, but it was too much rain to travel in comfort. The tired windshield wipers on our car were barely adequate for us to see by. I was in the front seat with the driver and noticed his eyes kept shutting. No amount of questioning could make him admit he was too tired to drive. However, a couple of very near misses helped me make up my mind to enforce a rest upon him. We located a roadside coffee house and encouraged him to have several cups of strong coffee before proceeding on to our hotel. Naturally, we passed the same overturned trucks, cars and dead animals, unchanged from what we has seen about eight hours earlier on our way to Agra.

Our "whistle stop" tour of India was over. In the morning we were back at the international airport, trying to find our way through their exit procedures. At least we didn't need to cross over to the other airport to get gas! While we were having so much trouble entering the country, it had been suggested to me that we should be engaging the services of a handling agent like everyone else does (meaning the Airlines). The local agent was "Air India," so I looked up their representative and asked for his help. First he said there was the matter of the fee. Ken was with me when we went to the Air India office to consult his tariff schedule. The agent looked it up and said that their minimum fee was seven fifty US and that we would fit into that minimum category. Ken said that he had that much cash in his pocket and that he would look after it. Something didn't sound right to me. That was far too cheap. I asked the agent to repeat the price. *He said "Seven hundred and fifty dollars per aeroplane, US." Ken and I nearly fainted.* The agent said he realized it was a little high but that they were a government airline and employees were not allowed to make any adjustments to their tariffs, for any reason.

We declined his services and went ahead on our own. Jim found out that the flight planning had to be done over at the other airport. We couldn't depart from that airport, however, because we couldn't clear customs and immigration there. Several hours of formalities were involved, even after the flight planning was complete, but I was consoled by the fact that the group had saved $1,500.00 in handling fees.

PAKISTAN

All four of us were tired of the confusion we were creating at the international airports. We decided, that if there was not something special to see or fuel required, we would overfly some of the countries in our path. Pakistan fell into the category of providing nothing new, so our flight plan from New Delhi was filed for a flight direct to Oman, via Karachi,Pakistan, but without landing in Pakistan. There were thunderstorms forecast for the route, but both planes had functioning stormscopes, so we felt that we could handle the flight without major incident. Jim and I went first and Tal and Ken took off fifteen minutes behind us.

On the way to Karachi, we encountered several thunderstorms but our stormscope capably indicated the route we should fly to avoid them. Tal had more of a problem with the storms. Fifteen minutes behind us, the situation was different, and he was forced to circumnavigate around several large and dangerous cells. As a result, he soon was running an hour behind us. Near Karachi,to avoid a storm cell, we also flew to the side of our course as we entered Pakistani airspace. When we called the controllers in Karachi to advise them where we were and that we would soon be overflying their airport, much to our dismay, we were ordered to land.

The controller also requested my overflight number. I read him the numbers from the letter of permission I had received some months before (albeit my permission was for a landing). I was advised that it was Friday, a holiday in Pakistan. All their files were locked up and I was being ORDERED to land. I pleaded that we were at 12,000 feet and that it would take a lot of fuel and time to get up there again after landing. Once more I received the same terse command, "You must land." *A mental image of one or more jet fighters being dispatched to escort us flashed through our minds, so we throttled back and started down as instructed.*

When we had landed and parked, a small truck transported us to the radar control building, where I was taken inside to meet the head controller. He was upset because he had no authorization for us and also because we had strayed slightly off course in the storm. He read my letter of authority, had me write a short paragraph about why we left the airway, and told me that we were free to continue our flight to Oman. Barely half an hour had gone by, and I thought we were now clear of the Pakistani authorities. As I left the office, I was told by another official that I owed them a landing fee. It was $12.00 US. I gave him $24.00 for myself and Tal and requested that he inform the tower that our companions need not land. After all, Tal's authority was also mentioned in the letter I showed and I had prepaid his landing fee. The Pakistanis had nothing to gain by making Tal land. *I was also desperately trying to save him from this latest administrative hassle. It didn't work. Tal and Ken were also forced to land.*

When we went to return to our planes, we were stopped by a customs official who explained, that when we entered the radar control building, we broke the customs barrier and now must clear customs and immigration with both aeroplanes. We also had to obtain a letter from the chief of police to the effect that we had not been convicted of any crime while we had been in the country. The fact that we had never been out of their sight didn't matter. We declined an offer from one disreputable character who wanted to provide us with some questionable help for $100.00 per aeroplane. We appointed Jim and Tal to do it for nothing. Ken and I decided to try and find some fuel. We did locate a supplier on the field who had one small truck with a tank in the back holding about 100 gallons of avgas. We split it between the aeroplanes. The split was approximate because the only measuring device available was an unmarked wooden stick. While we were out fueling up the planes, I noticed that each passenger aeroplane parked on the airport was ringed by eight soldiers armed with automatic rifles. They all stood facing away from the plane they were guarding, and both provisioning and baggage trucks approaching the planes were rigidly inspected. When a plane landed, a new group of soldiers marched out and were placed on guard around it. *I was convinced that we had made the right decision to forego a Pakistan sightseeing stop on our trip. It was also obviously correct to have complied with their order, ''You Must Land!''*

A long five hours after landing, we were ready for departure. It was beginning to get dark, and we had previously decided against night flying in this part of the world. We had a choice to make. We could either fly on to Oman, crossing the corner of Iranian airspace at night, or stay overnight and struggle with a new barrage of Pakistani paperwork before departure in the morning. The thought of getting another clearance from the police chief helped us make up our mind. We took off into the setting Pakistani sun.

Our night flight to Oman was uneventful – until our arrival, at

11:30 P.M. As soon as we landed and were parked on their otherwise unoccupied apron, the assistant duty manager came out to greet us and arrange for our fuel. *When he discovered that we didn't have visas for Oman, his attitude cooled and he advised us that we would have to go on to some other airport since we couldn't stay in Oman without visas.* He was suggesting that we proceed out over the Persian Gulf, after midnight, through one of the world's most active military areas, to Bahrain. We could have fuel but we couldn't stay overnight!

I remembered Ken had requested visas for Oman, in Washington, D.C. several months before. He went to the Oman consulate and was told by a receptionist that we didn't need to get visas ahead of time because they would be issued at the airport in Oman on arrival. The assistant duty manager said that was true, except that this was Friday, their religious holiday, and no visas are issued on Fridays. I called for the duty manager and advised him , in no uncertain terms, that it was their employee in Washington that was remiss by not advising us of the Friday restriction. I then barked at him that *we were not going anywhere!* We had had enough! It was now after midnight and we had been up since five AM and hassled by one individual or another since shortly after that. In addition, the temperature was still about 100 degrees and I was beat.

We were eventually invited into the terminal, provided we sat on a row of chairs just inside the door. At least it was air-conditioned. While we waited, I read that Oman was very poor until oil was discovered there in 1970. The country's economy is now based on oil and fish, but mostly on oil. Before 1970, there were only nine hundred children in school and they were all boys. Now there are over 250,000 children receiving an education and half of them are girls.

The young airport duty manager took part in closed- door meetings with several Arabs in offices across the room from us, and then returned triumphantly. They had contacted a big boss, having his religious holiday dinner at home, and received special permission for us to enter the country for the night on a restricted visa. The actual town of Muscat is located about thirty miles from the airport. Our permission was only valid to travel to the airport hotel one mile away, stay the night, and leave in the morning. *That suited us just fine. I slept like a log.*

16

The Ultimate Challenge

THE MIDDLE EAST

"Are you hit?"
"Yes, But I think I can make it back to Shiraz (an airport in Iran)."
"Okay, I'll let them know you are trying to get there and will need help if you do."

This was the substance of the radio conversation we intercepted between two Iranian fighter pilots as we flew over the Persian Gulf between Abu Dhabi, in the United Arab Emerates, and Bahrain. A few miles back, the controller had warned all aircraft in his sector not to use the international emergency frequency of 121.5 MHZ, because it was busy. **Naturally we tuned in immediately!** What we heard was excited Persian chatter, but I could tell from the urgency in their voices, that someone was in serious trouble.

When the excitement subsided, Tal called from the other plane to translate for us. He had taken his medical degree in Geneva many years before and had boarded with a young man from Persia (Iran) for some time. From this association, he understood Persian and still remembered enough to discern the substance of those frantic transmissions.

Tal spoke several languages. He was born in Turkey and, in his early years, spoke only Turkish. When he decided to become a doctor, he began studying English and used his new language for all his correspondence to potential schools throughout Europe. Eventually, he decided on the medical school in Geneva, Switzerland. All his replies from them had been in English so he assumed this would be the language of instruction. He left home in Istanbul, with his High School diploma and a Turkish - English dictionary in his knapsack, and reported for his first class. There he got an even bigger surprise than the one we had just experienced. *All his lectures for the next six years were to be in FRENCH!*

Nine people out of ten would have gone right back home. Tal registered for night classes in French at the Berlitz Language School. He went to his university lectures to learn what he could from the pictures and then read up on the day's courses in English at the public library, when he could find time. Gradually, he began to comprehend more and more from the French lectures, made the transition and completed his medical degree in French. Tal was a very useful person to have along with his knowledge of Turkish, French, English, Persian and perhaps a few others. He later completed his Cardiology training in Pittsburgh, Pennsylvania, but I don't think that was as much of a challenge for him. After all, when he attended his first lecture in the Pittsburgh, he was already familiar with the language!

Below us passed several warships and oil tankers. The controllers in the Middle East airspace are almost all British, and their expertise was greatly appreciated after some of the less proficient handling we had experienced in the third world. The controllers had us pinpointed on their radar throughout our flight and cautioned us to stay right in the center of the designated airway, for our own safety. *The whole Persian Gulf control area was charged with tension, and we did not need any coaxing to stay on course.*

At the end of this sensitive three hour flight, we landed on the tiny Sheikdom island of Bahrain, fourteen miles off the Saudi Arabian coast. Manama, the capital city, has a population of 175,000, roughly half the population of Bahrain. Bahrain is considered the Singapore of the Middle East. It has been independent since 1971, after 150 years as a British protectorate. It is oil-rich, yet prices are high. There is essentially no unemployment and education and medical care are free. However, aircraft handling is not!

The handlers wanted $75.00 per plane to guide us through the Bahrain paperwork, but we convinced them that two little Twin Comanches barely equaled one larger plane, and were awarded a group rate. While Jim, Tal and I accomplished the administrative functions in most cities we visited, Ken spent his time researching hotels and possible tours. He performed well and booked us into the Gulf Hotel. Most of the major hotel chains were represented in Bahrain, but Ken's choice overlooked the Sheik's palace. It was a sight to behold and bespoke the language of recent, vast wealth.

Sheik's New Forest — Bahrain.

As I stood looking out of our hotel window, to my left was the palace. In front of me was a man–made forest consisting of thousands of freshly planted, irrigated trees. The forest was surrounded by a high stone fence several miles long with a post and light atop it every few feet. There must have been a thousand lights on that fence. To my right, was a magnificent Mosque. The Sheik could go out his front door and walk through his personal forest into his Mosque. All of this was on an island that, without oil money, would still be a desert.

Our $75.00 had been well spent. In the morning our handlers whisked us through the airport routine in short order. There was an hour and a half delay but it was our own fault. Once again, our economical military approach plate book was without plates for Riyadh, Saudi Arabia. A set was finally located, and two hours later we landed in the Saudi Arabian capital for some of its low-priced fuel. I had been told by the crew of the "Odyssey," a DC3, that had circled the globe a year earlier, that they paid approximately 35 cents per gallon for fuel in Saudi Arabia. I felt we should make the same pit stop and drink in as much of this inexpensive fuel as we could, as the price was approximately one tenth of what we had been paying in most countries.

There was no air traffic as we approached the desert airport at Riyadh, so I was surprised to see **two** parallel runways, both 13,000 feet in length. We were cleared to land on the right hand runway and directed into the general aviation terminal. There, I learned what the other runway was for – the exclusive use of the King! He also had his own terminal building beside his personal runway. Oil wells can buy many things!

Mecca, Saudi Arabia is the birthplace of the Prophet Mohammed, and the birthplace of the Islamic religion. Alcohol and drugs are, therefore, strictly prohibited, and possession of either is punishable by a lengthy jail sentence. Weekly holidays in Islam are Thursday and Friday, but fortunately, it was now Saturday, a normal working day.

I enquired from the handlers about the price of fuel. They assured me it was very cheap, around 25 cents per gallon. I told them to arrange for the fuel company fill it up my tanks. *When I received the invoice from the fuel company, the actual price was $3.60 per gallon. It proved useless to argue with an Arab in 120 degree heat on his own turf?* The price remained as invoiced and they added landing and handling fees to boot. I was pretty sure I was being "taken," but there was nothing more I could do about it. I reluctantly paid the bill. The handlers then flight planned us for 12,000 feet, the highest and coolest altitude we could fly without using supplemental oxygen, and we took off for Luxor in southern Egypt.

The runways at Riyadh are 13,000 feet long for a good reason. In this extreme desert heat the takeoff roll is much longer than normal, and the rate of climb, once the aircraft is off the ground, is terrible. In a Twin Comanche, obtaining altitude is best described as like "milking a mouse." In the noonday sun we had to "step-climb" all the way up. This is because the aeroplane travels slower during a climb, and air-cooled engines overheat. Every thousand feet we had to level off, speed up, and cool down the engines. This process was repeated many times before we reached our flight planned altitude. At 12,000 feet there was finally some relief from the torturous temperatures of ground level.

As we crossed the Arabian desert, the landscape below us was the most desolate we saw on the trip. Dry sand and rocks kept passing in review. We saw no water of any kind. It seemed, no one could possibly live there, but apparently they did. We passed two tiny settlements of mud huts. We never saw any people outside their tiny dwellings, but then why would they come out into that murderous sun?

EGYPT, A LAND OF HISTORY

Upon crossing the Red Sea we entered Egypt. Egypt has been described as a large brown package tied with a slender green ribbon. The ribbon, of course, is the greenery that surrounds the Nile river. The rest is desert. Herodotus said, "Egypt is the gift of the Nile." The Nile is one of the longest rivers in the world, and is truly the life blood of Egypt. Our first destination was Luxor, four hundred miles south of Cairo. For many centuries Luxor was called Thebes and was the center of Egypt, both its capital and its heart. Nowhere else in the world has time left such a great heritage of ancient civilizations so intact as the monuments in Luxor. It is a marvel that, in this historic city, almost every single stone has a story to tell.

The airport at Luxor is small and handles both national and international traffic. Our entry into Egypt was made easy because of the assistance we received from our own personal soldier guide. We simply showed him the digital watch he was to receive when we were clear of the airport, and he helped us accomplish all our formalities in less than an hour. We prepaid the police chief for the young military guard he positioned between our aircraft, and selected our taxi driver from among a large group of idle men clamoring for our business.

We chose correctly. At six feet, four inches, and over two hundred pounds, Mohammed was an imposing figure. He spoke English well and had an air conditioned station wagon. He was pleasant and knowledgeable. He became our personal attendant from the time we arrived until he waved to us as we departed the next evening. *When we left our belongings in his open vehicle to visit an attraction, I asked him why he didn't lock it. He replied, "No one in Luxor touches Mohammed's car!", and he meant it.*

We checked into the picturesque "Sheraton On The Nile." It was perfect. They accepted us at air crew rates and gave us rooms facing the Nile. We watched authentic Felucca boats ply the river with their versatile sail and looked across the Nile to the "City of the Dead." The sunset was a sight to behold as it cast its long, dark shadows on that famous river in front of us, and then silently slipped behind the rugged mountains beyond. In the relative cool of the evening, we set out for the Karnak Temples to see their show of light and sound. Amidst all those colossal statues, we learned about a previous time. When the show was over, we wandered amongst the people of Luxor. They were on the streets in large numbers till late at night. During the summer in Egypt, the people are outside from very early in the morning until about eleven AM.

Baking bread inside a Luxor home.

Native people then go to their homes, where most of them have an electric fan, and try to stay cool. In late afternoon, they venture forth once again. Tourists go back to their hotels and alternate between their air–conditioned rooms and the swimming pool.

Egyptian women wear black outside the home. Note the old and new generation water containers.

We asked Mohammed why all the women on the streets were dressed in black. He told us they wear black outside of their homes so that they will not look appealing to other men. Within their own home, they often wear bright colors and try to look as attractive as they can. I also noticed that, while the older ladies transport water in the traditional earthenware jugs, the youngsters now carry it in plastic bottles discarded by the tourists. Nearly every tourist in the area carries one of these plastic bottles, filled with cold, distilled water, as they tour in the hot Egyptian sun.

Mohammed met us in the morning at 5:00 AM and took us to the ferry which crosses the Nile to the West bank and the "City of the Dead." While we waited for the ferry, several men came to the river with their horses. They waded into the water with their steeds and had their morning bath together. Then both emerged from the muddy water, dripped dry, and went about their daily routine.

Men and their horses bathe together in the Nile before commencing daily routine in Luxor.

Hand packing cars on the ferry — Luxor.

The loading of the ferry was far from routine. When the ferry arrived, no one ashore would yield space for unloading, so it took twice as long as it should to exit. Then all the waiting cars and trucks scrambled for position somewhere on the ferry. Anywhere would do!. When the ferry was unable to take more cars, it was obvious that it was not really full. There were still lots of half and quarter spaces between vehicles. The shouting started and everyone accused one another of stupidity. Mohammed finally took charge, and it was like magic! He commanded an aura of respect. The men worked for him in groups, hand packing the cars closer together on the ferry, until there was room for all the vehicles still waiting on shore. It seemed to me that, wherever he moved, "the mountain came to Mohammed." We crossed the river peacefully and then the scramble to exit the ferry happened all over again on the other side.

Entrance (in foreground) to King Tut's Tomb in the Valley of the Kings.

The "City of the Dead" has three major areas – the Valley of the Kings, the Valley of the Queens, and the tombs of the nobles. The Valley of the Kings has over 60 tombs of Pharoahs and noblemen. We began our tour with one of the most famous tombs, that of King Tut Ankh Amon. It was discovered in 1922 by professor Howard Carter from England, and is the only Pharonic tomb to have escaped intact the plundering of the tomb robbers. As you can see from the picture, the entrance is small and the tomb is located under the entrance of another, larger tomb. That unusual location is the reason it was never found earlier and robbed like all the others.

King Tut's tomb is small in comparison to other Pharaoh's because he died at the age of eighteen, having reigned only nine years. When a man first became Pharaoh, construction of his tomb commenced. If, for example, he ruled for sixty years there was time to build him a large elaborate tomb, complete with false chambers to mislead any robbers. It could also have many rooms for the things he would need to take with him for his use in the afterlife. Tut's tomb has but one main chamber. From the riches that were found in and around this single burial chamber, one can imagine what treasures must have been robbed from the tombs of the long lived Pharaohs before him.

The boy king's tomb still contains a golden sarcophagus guarded by twelve apes painted on the wall above his head, to protect him during the twelve hours of darkness each night. On the side wall is a colorful mural depicting King Tut going to the

The Weighing Of The Heart.
Shown here, printed on real original style papyrus paper, is the ceremony of the weighing of the heart. This mythical ceremony was performed with the deceased's heart to determine if he or she would go to Heaven or Hell. On the left of the scale, the tray contains feathers — on the right, the deceased's heart. If the feathers weigh more than the heart, (signifying an honorable life) the deceased goes to Heaven. If the heart weighs more than the feathers, (signifying a dishonorable life) the dog beside the scale gets to eat the heart and the deceased goes to Hell. The priest is shown holding the departed's hand, awaiting the result.

after life and his wife marrying the high priest. The colors are still brilliant. This brought up an interesting question. How did they illuminate the underground tombs when they painted the walls in the fourteenth century? The workmen couldn't use oil lamps, because the smoke would dull the brilliance of the colors. Instead, they used mirrors! Since the sun shines all day in Luxor, a series of mirrors were positioned, reflecting rays of light down corridors and around corners, until it reached the area being painted. Our guides supplied an actual demonstration to prove how this was possible.

Later we travelled farther inland to the Temple of Queen Hatshepsut in the Valley of the Queens. It was above ground, built as a series of grand terraces extending up a rock wall, with rows of granite columns blending in with the mountainside. Active restoration of this temple resumes each winter by hired stone workers, imported from Poland, who have indexed and catalogued the rubble in preparation for the restoration. By the time we finished viewing this site, it was noon so we returned to our hotel for our air-conditioned siesta.

Toward the end of the afternoon, we drove to the airport for our evening departure to Cairo. We had decided to make this flight at night to gain another day and also to travel in the coolest part of the day. We didn't want to have to step-climb the aircraft again, if we could avoid it. Mohammed easily helped us with our paperwork at the airport. Everyone seemed to know and respect him. If I were to go back to Luxor, he would be the first person I'd look up.

CAIRO

The controller at Luxor airport didn't request our special military clearance for flight within Egypt from his superiors until we had taxied for takeoff. As a result we sat at the end of the runway, waiting for this special clearance, for nearly half an hour. While we waited, Jim noticed concrete bunkers near the end of the runway, that housed fighter planes in bomb- proof shelters. These planes could be retrieved from their underground locations, and take to the air in defence of Egypt, at a moment's notice. This small airport was more important than it first appeared. Finally, our military clearance arrived and we flew north to Cairo.

It was late at night when we arrived in this city of fifteen million people and a million lights. As we approached the Cairo airport, we could see one long, wide, inky black strip through the center of the city lights below us. It was the Nile as it widens out to a delta, near the Mediterranean Sea, a few miles to the north. We landed at their international airport, and not wanting to try and find our own way around this monstrous place in the dark, hired their handlers to look after us. Once again, we stayed at a Sheraton near the airport at air crew rates.

Remains of the 9 pyramids of Giza. Note the alabaster top on the largest pyramid.

At 6:00 A.M. we were in a car headed for the Pyramids of Giza. This group of pyramids, together with the Sphinx, comprise one of the seven wonders of the ancient world. They are in fact, the only ancient wonder still in existence. The pyramids were constructed 4,000 years ago of granite rocks quarried in the hills above Cairo. The huge stones were floated to the site in boats on the Nile. Ropes were then used to pull them up to the construction site. The granite was originally covered with an alabaster protective layer. However, this alabaster was later permanently borrowed for the construction of the Citadel, a beautiful mosque built by the original Mohammed Ali, in the centre of Cairo.

The author astride his Cairo camel.

At the pyramids, we rented camels for the long, circular, ride around the site. When we reached the smallest of the three major pyramids, the Pyramid of Chephren, there was a climbing guide waiting to escort young volunteers to the top. Tal and I voted for

Jim atop the Pyramid of Chephren.

Jim to represent our group atop the pyramid, and away he went. The rest of us sat in the shade of the pyramid below and watched him climb all those three-foot steps to the peak. Following this, we rode the camels to a dune out in the desert from where we could get the best view of all nine remaining Pyramids of Gisa. As we came closer to this isolated desert location, I noticed an Arab sitting beside a tiny tent. Pondering why he was there, I discovered he was selling ice cold Coke from a cooler inside the tent for one dollar a bottle. He had a completely captive market and anxious customers. *Before leaving home for a visit to the pyramids, there is one technique that should be practiced. Jim and I found it very difficult to change the film in our cameras while riding a bouncing camel!*

Following a sweltering morning on the desert, it felt good to get back to the hotel for a swim and rest. Later in the afternoon, we went downtown to the banks of the Nile searching for a Felucca boat ride. When I saw a seasoned looking middle-aged captain beside a good looking Felucca, I negotiated a price for the four of us, and we boarded for a one hour sunset sail. *Then our real captain showed up. He was about twelve years old. His first mate was about ten.* The man we had been dealing with was the owner, but he no longer took tourists out on the river. However, there was nothing to worry about. Those two young men knew their boat and the river by heart. They had us back where we started, within five minutes of the hour, without a watch.

17

The Ultimate Challenge

EUROPE

Tal was anxious to get home. He had been talking to his office, and his partners wanted to leave for their vacations as soon as possible. After a meeting on our last night in Cairo, we resolved to go directly to Geneva and have the aircraft serviced there for the final ocean flights over the North Atlantic. Tal would show us around Geneva, and then we would fly straight home.

This was acceptable, for the montage of countries already visited was beginning to blur. Besides, I had seen most of Europe many years before from my motorcycle. I had hoped to add visits to Cyprus, Greece and Turkey during Circum '87, but these countries would have to wait until another year.

We expected a smooth exit from Cairo because we knew that we had handlers to help us. *As usual, this did not work exactly according to plan.* We had arrived in Cairo at night and were not able to make a proper assessment of the airport layout before leaving for our hotel. We didn't know that there were two terminals! At the airport, we tried everywhere to locate our handlers without success. An hour later, we found out that we were in Terminal two, and they were in Terminal one. This may sound a little like Toronto, Canada, to some people. We took a taxi to the other terminal. We usually fueled up upon arrival, but our late night landing in Cairo had caused us to modify our routine and leave this until our departure. Our handlers were able to grease the administrative wheels *but proved hopeless at getting us fuel.*

After an interminable wait at the planes, the head fuel man arrived to check out our proposed method of payment, before dispatching a fuel truck. When he was satisfied, he returned to his depot, somewhere distant on the airport, and sent us a fuel truck – with JET FUEL! The driver, of course, spoke no English and even Tal couldn't converse with him in Egyptian. In due course, we convinced him that we couldn't use the fuel in his truck, and he went back to his depot with our note requesting aviation gasoline. When the ancient little gas truck finally did arrive, its delivery pump was faulty. It either wouldn't pump or it pumped far too fast. I was hesitant to even put my thoughts into words in case they ignited the gas fumes, which were everywhere. Clearly, the worst part of flying through so many different countries was the amount of time we spent in non-productive activity at International airports. *Certainly, the one attribute that I was forced to develop as I travelled was* **PATIENCE!**

Instead of taking off in the relative cool of the early morning, we departed six hours late at high noon. The weather was clear, and luckily our departure path took us right over top of the pyramids of Giza. I was surprised at how much smaller they looked from only 4,000 feet and how close they were to the edge of Cairo.

We passed over the island of Crete and the southern tip of Greece as we winged across the Mediterranean Sea to Italy. The controllers along the way didn't seem to understand that a small plane like ours, flying at a mere 10,000 feet, could be on an instrument flight plan. We were directed to climb to 10,500 feet which is a visual flight altitude. As we approached Italy, we were criticized for flying at that height and ordered back down to 10,000 feet. There doesn't appear to be the same degree of communication between controllers from different countries in this part of the world that we have come to expect here in North America.

After eight hours in the air, we arrived in Brindisi, Italy, a small seaport town on the East side of the Italian boot, just as it was becoming dark. Brindisi is an air force base and naval center. Tourists often travel there by train and then take a boat to Greece.

Our hotel was probably the oldest and most expensive we experienced on the trip. Its elevator was sized for two people at a time – perhaps three, if they knew each other very well. There were no air crew rates because there were usually no air crews there. But there was Pasta!

We had a true Italian dinner, complete with local wine, and walked to the town square by the harbor. There must have been 10,000 people outside in the pleasant evening air. They were watching a movie on a giant outdoor screen by the water. The feature was "ROCKY IV" with Italian subtitles.

The following morning, I was requested by the authorities to make a thorough check of my communication radios, before take-off. The tower had experienced difficulty in hearing us on our arrival the evening before. The test proved one radio to be well below standard. This caused me no concern for I had brought along an extra identical radio just in case this happened. I made the switch, and my takeoff restriction was lifted.

With our flight planning completed, we attempted to pay our landing fees. The airport, however, charged by the hour for parking, so we were instructed to gas up first and return to pay the fees immediately prior to taking off. Fuel is rationed in that area, and the fuel dealer had to get signed authority before he could sell us any. I think the airport office knew there was going to be some delay, which is why they wouldn't estimate our takeoff time and allow us to prepay our parking accordingly. We eventually received our fuel and went back to the airport office. NOW, they told us they could only take payment in Lira! They could not accept credit cards, travellers cheques or American cash. It was suggested that we go to the bank in the airport terminal building to obtain the local currency. The longer we took to get it, the more Lira we would require to pay our ever-increasing hourly parking fees.

There was one girl at the bank. She said her bank never takes travellers cheques but that she had exchanged some American cash into Lira just yesterday. She offered to phone and get the current exchange rate. I couldn't understand what she was saying on the phone, but I could tell from the look in her eyes that things were not going well. She hung up and apologetically explained that their bank was not accepting U.S. money that day. The only place I could obtain the Lira I required, was at a bank in the town center, several miles away. *Now, I not only had to estimate how much I required for the airport fees, I also had to include enough to pay for the round trip taxi fare!* There was no way I could estimate all this exactly so I exchanged more than I required and returned, pockets bulging with Lira, to buy our way out of the Brindisi airport.

Once again, after an early morning start, it was five minutes past noon before we became airborne. The weather was clear and we flew at 12,000 feet past Rome, Florence and Venice toward Geneva, Switzerland. As we flew northward, the hills began to form into mountains and the minimum en route altitudes increased, first to 14,000 feet, then to 16,000 and finally to 18,000 feet. We began breathing supplemental oxygen through our nasal cannulas. The cannula is a hospital type breathing device that feeds oxygen through a small plastic tube up each nostril. It is much more efficient then a mask, using only about one fifth the amount of oxygen. It also permits talking, eating and drinking while breathing the enriched air–oxygen mixture through the nose. The cannulas Jim and I were using are only certified to 18,000 feet. Above that, the security of a full mask is required. This altitude restriction has not been a problem for us, as 18,000 feet is all that is required to cross most mountain ranges or to climb over marginal weather.

The Swiss Alps in August.

As we approached Geneva, the snow and beautiful white glaciers on the Swiss Alps were alongside us. We were within 2,000 feet of the peaks. Even a mountain climber doesn't get to see the panoramic views that we did on that flight. After crossing the last escarpment, down below us in the valley was Lake Geneva. In the crystal clear mountain air, the city of Geneva was visible at the end of the lake, over seventy-five miles away.

The controllers directed us through several large circular let-downs over the valley until we were low enough to commence our approach into the Geneva airport. The approach toward this lovely city is breathtaking. As we came closer, we passed a huge fountain, on the edge of Lake Geneva, shooting a stream of water hundreds of feet into the air. There was so much to see that it was difficult to concentrate on our flying.

On the ground, the immigration and customs officials just waved us a friendly "hello." There were no general declaration forms required. We were out of the third world and back in civilization! It was really a welcome feeling. Instead of our average five hour trek through the paper jungle, we were cleared in five minutes.

Tal had lived in Geneva for over six years when he was a medical student, so naturally he was in charge. He explained that periodically, as a student, he had been suspended from his regular residence quarters for various youthful misconducts. During those intervals of minor disgrace, he stayed at a small hotel called the Air Escali. Since it was close to the airport, we stayed there as well. It was far from new but was well kept, and the charming young lady at the desk, Beatrice, was a pilot.

Beatrice was not only a desk clerk and part time pilot. She was also a morning radio sports announcer. She spoke perfect English and French. Beatrice also spoke the language of pilots and gave us a discount on our rooms. She got off work at 7 P.M. and agreed to accompany us to dinner and be our guide for the evening. Tal and Beatrice selected another of his old haunts, the Cafe de Paris, for dinner.

While the other four ordered, I went in search of a phone. I needed to make an overseas call back home to the local newspaper to file my periodic progress report. By the time I had successfully completed my call and returned to the restaurant, they were all having their dessert. They told me they had taken the liberty of pre–ordering an excellent choice for me and waved to the waiter to bring me my entree. With a flourish the waiter approached with my plate held high above his head. *When it reached the table I knew I had been ''had.'' It was a McDonalds hamburger! My delicious steak arrived soon thereafter.*

We spent the next day at the airport having our aircraft serviced for the final time. Before we headed out over the North Atlantic for Canada, we wanted to be certain that everything was right. Tal had a faulty gyro on his HSI. However, a new one was readily available in Geneva. Clearly, this was the city in which to make our maintenance stop. Once the planes were ready, a vote was taken, and it was decided that we would stay in Geneva an extra day for sightseeing.

Beatrice contacted a girl friend of hers named Helen. The six of us travelled across the border into France and took a cablecar up to the restaurant atop Saleve mountain. We sat at a large window table overlooking Geneva and watched the sparkling lights of the city over dinner. Helen invited all of us to her apartment the following evening to witness the fireworks display that marks the end of the annual Festival of Geneva, which was to take place while we were there.

The next day, it was Tal's turn to be our tour guide. First, we toured the League of Nations buildings and grounds. There was a feeling of hopelessness about the concept in this age of perpetual conflict around the world. He took us to old Geneva, with its cobblestone streets, high on the hill. The buildings dated back to 1,500 AD, and many had signs on them telling of their occupancy by noted personages of that era. We also toured new Geneva and had lunch by the waterfront, in a colorful sidewalk cafe.

The people of Geneva all seemed to be prospering. They had to be for most of the goods in the stores cost more than they do in the United States. During the past few days, we had travelled from abject poverty to a land of plenty. Money, of course, is what Switzerland is all about. I was well aware of the numbered Swiss bank accounts that abound in this country, but I also learned something else. They will exchange almost any currency! This was what we had been waiting for. We gathered up all our remaining money from Brindisi, and all the other countries we had visited, and took it to the bank. The

Changing leftover currencies for Swiss Francs in Geneva.

expressions on our faces in the picture indicate how happy we were to trade all our leftover change for Swiss francs.

That evening, we went to Helen's apartment to have a barbecue and see the fireworks from her balcony. The fireworks

Beatrice (L) and Helen (R) with Circum '87 crews just before Fête de Genève fireworks display.

display we watched that evening was clearly the finest I have ever seen. As if by magic, just before the fireworks began, the city turned dark. The city fathers had pulled the big switch and darkened all the streets so that the effect of the fireworks would be appreciated to its maximum. The show was also synchronized to music. Since it was impossible to have loudspeakers large enough to spread sound throughout all of Geneva, they simply played the music over the radio stations. We listened to the sound track with a portable radio on the balcony. It was certainly our good fortune to be in Geneva on that particular day of the year. We were also lucky to have stayed at Tal's favorite old hotel and met Beatrice, the desk clerk, pilot, sports announcer and now, friend.

Beatrice flying her Swiss–registered aeroplane beside the famous Matterhorn mountain.

In the morning, while we were fueling the planes for a full day of flying, Beatrice came to say good bye. She also brought me a picture of herself in her Swiss registered aeroplane flying beside Mount Matterhorn in the snow–covered Alps. Just before we enplaned, I learned of another practice in Geneva that I approve of. When people kiss good–bye they kiss three times. They kiss one cheek, the other cheek and then the first cheek again. It's a great custom!

Heading Northward, we climbed out of the valley of Geneva, and traversed the fields of France. Many years before I had passed by these same fields on my motorcycle. Things looked entirely different now, flying over them at nearly two hundred miles per hour. The fields had lost their individual personalities, appearing practically flat in a checkerboard of yellows and greens.

We crossed the English Channel and there below us, glistening in the sun, were the white cliffs of Dover. Two years before, Jim and I had flown over England but cloud had obscured our view. This time it was clear and we could see everything. Heathrow airport and London with all its parks, passed below. Soon we were over water again, but this time it was the Irish Sea. The sea gave way to lush green fields, and we encountered some light rain. We were in Ireland. Five hours from Geneva, we landed at Shannon, Ireland, for lunch and reflected on the many accents we had heard in that short flight. Departing Geneva, we spoke to a Swiss-German controller, then a Frenchman, an Englishman and finally an Irishman. *They were all speaking English to us as we crossed their sectors but they all sounded very, very different.*

18

The Ultimate Challenge

THE NORTH ATLANTIC

From Shannon, Ireland, we flew to Reykjavik, Iceland. It was easier than it had been two years ago, coming home from the New York to Paris Air Rally. We could now carry much more fuel. We no longer had to make a fuel stop at Vagar in the Faeroe Islands, because the five hour estimated flight time to Iceland was now well within our capabilities. Victor Koss, back in Oakland, was right. Having lots of fuel makes flight planning easier and then flying your flight plan safer. When I arrived home I planned to have the remaining ferry tank removed and the back seats replaced. The new tip tanks, with their two extra hours of fuel, however, were NEVER coming off the plane!

About half way to Reykjavik, we encountered cloudy skies and began to pick up ice on the airframe and propellors. We had travelled through some of the hottest climates in the world but now we were headed north to the Arctic circle. A simple adjustment in altitude took our plane out of that hostile, ice laden environment, and we reached the Icelandic capital without incident. We arrived well before dark, for the sun at this latitude doesn't set until after 10:30 P.M., even in the latter part of August. After fueling, I attempted to show Ken the nightspots Jim and I had visited two years earlier. Unfortunately, it was Sunday night and they were all closed. That was unlucky for Ken because the young men on the Air Rally had described the Icelandic ladies as friendly and anxious to meet touring pilots. *In fact one of the young pilots had described the situation as ''like shooting fish in a barrel.''*

Reykjavík, Iceland.

Reykjavik is the most north'erly capital in the world. It is extraordinarily fortunate in having a clean and cheap source of heat in the form of geothermal energy. Until 1930 the city's inhabitants had little benefit from this natural resource. In that year the hot water was first harnessed and distributed to a hospital, school and about seventy houses. Since then, technology has progressed and deep wells have been drilled. Now, there is sufficient hot water to heat all of Reykjavik and still sell some surplus to neighboring municipalities and even heat some of the streets.

Another interesting custom in Iceland prevents family names from being handed down from one generation to another. When a child is born he or she is given a first name only. The child, if a boy, can later choose a surname by adding the suffix ''son'' to either his father's or his mother's first name. Thus ,if Thor and Helen had a son and named him John, the son could select either Thorson or Helenson for his last name. (The boy usually opted to add ''son'' to his father's first name while it was common for a girl to add "dottir" to her mother's.) In the next generation the son of John Thorson would have the last name of Johnson. No child born in Iceland, would ever automatically benefit from a famous family surname like Kennedy, Rockefeller or Roosevelt.

When an Icelandic–born boy left the country for the United States or Canada, the surname he departed with was retained and handed down from generation to generation according to the custom of his new land. The girls surname disappeared when she adopted her North American husband's name upon marriage. When we look in the phone book and see all those surnames like Davidson, Jackson or Thompson, we are most likely reading about families that came originally from Iceland. The surprising fact is that most of those families in North America with surnames ending in "son", were spawned from an Icelandic population that, even today, numbers under 250,000 people.

That night, we stayed in the Hotel Loftleidir located right on the airport. *There are not many cities in the world where you can park your plane within only one hundred yards of your hotel room.* Because of the location and the easy administration at this airport, we had one of our best morning starts of the trip. The plan was to take off for Greenland at 7:30 A.M. and Jim and I pushed our throttles forward at 7:37.

The North Atlantic hadn't changed in the last two years. The water below was still only one or two degrees above freezing. Large, blue–white icebergs dotted the hostile seas beneath us. Jim and I went over our ditching drill. *If it should become necessary to put the plane down in that cold water, we would have only one or two minutes to get into the raft before we became immobilized by the cold.* The good news was that the tail winds were considerably stronger than forcasted. Flying on economy fuel settings we were able to average better than 165 knots, or 190 MPH, over the water.

I decided we could easily make it all the way to Goose Bay in Labrador without stopping in Greenland at all. Jim, Tal and Ken all cross–checked my calculations and agreed. I checked to make sure that I had the approach plates, in the cockpit with me, for Goose Bay. I did, so we passed by the southern tip of Greenland without landing and headed for Canada. We had just saved a pair of $60.00

U.S. landing fees, buying fuel at $6.00 U.S. per gallon and at least a two hour stopover.

As we neared the Canadian coast, we ran into skies laden with solid cloud and flew toward Labrador with the two aircraft safely separated by altitude. I made a thorough study of the instrument landing approach plates and studied our most probable instrument approach. *Then the power went out in Goose Bay! Their radar and all the navigation aids went off the air.* The emergency power cut in and activated the voice communication channels and one navigational aid, their ADF. All the arriving aircraft were directed to perform a race-track shaped holding pattern above the ADF beacon at different altitudes. When Jim and I entered our hold, there were four planes stacked below us. As each plane completed its landing, all the aircraft in the pattern were dropped 1000 feet and the lowest one authorized to approach and land.

When our turn arrived, we flew the full procedure ADF approach pattern and started down toward the runway. At 1000 feet above ground we broke out of the cloud and rain. There was Canada in front of us! I hadn't seen North America in nearly two months. We landed and Tal landed right behind us. We exchanged congratulatory handshakes and reflected on the score to date. Both planes were safely back on the North American continent. *Our ocean flying was finished for this trip and the final score, after spending more than 100 hours out over four oceans of the world, was ''Humans 4 – Sharks 0''.*

19

The Ultimate Challenge

WELCOME HOME

The hotel in Goose Bay was probably the most basic of all the hotels we stayed in on the trip. There was little to hold us there in the morning. Flight planning and fueling were quick and easy. The weather at daybreak was fair as we departed for Timmins, Ontario. We had flight planned as a two–aircraft "flight" once again and flew over the Quebec wilderness side by side in the brilliant morning sunshine. In just under seven hours, we landed at Timmins for lunch and fuel.

In the early afternoon, we were back in the air headed across Ontario and the corner of Lake Superior for Thunder Bay, Ontario. The conversations between our aircraft became light and casual, for we were back where we felt at home in the air. Navigation was relaxed and easy. We now knew that we were going to complete this flight successfully. Both aircraft were performing perfectly, and the friendly controller's voices sounded like music to our ears.

It was late afternoon when we got to Thunder Bay. We decided to overnight there and proceed to Winnipeg in the morning. For the final time on our trip, we flashed our pilots cards and flight suits at the front desk of the hotel and obtained our air crew discount. It had been a long day of flying but we were all in good spirits.

I telephoned the newspaper for whom I had written over the past two months. I also called the radio show host who had interviewed me before I left. I provided both of them with our estimated arrival time, just before noon the following day.

We awoke to a clear blue sky and a bright sun. We were only two and a half hours from home. Time seemed to move slowly. We took to the air as a formation "flight" again, keeping in sight of each other and talking constantly between the two planes. We hardly shut up all the way home! All those interminable delays at third world airports now seemed worthwhile. Jim was relaxed. Tal was smiling and Ken game me a "thumbs up" sign across the short stretch of sky between our planes. As we neared Winnipeg, I requested permission for a two aircraft formation fly-past down the active runway on our arrival. The controller asked me how many hours we had flown on the trip and how many miles we covered. I answered him with 154 hours and 26,000 miles. Our fly-past was approved.

When we got closer to the airport, I informed the tower that both planes would fly down the runway side by side at minimum altitude. I would then break right and circle to land. Tal would break to the left, make a larger circle and land behind me. I had always wanted to do that but had never been given the opportunity. It was a great way to end the flight. Jim and I shook hands as we turned off the runway.

Taxiing in, the ground controller advised that one taxiway had been blocked off for us and the television cameras were waiting there. Never had four part-time pilots felt more pleased or important. Following television pictures and interviews, we continued our taxi in to the parking ramp, where a small group of well-wishers had gathered with red carpets, welcome home balloons and chilled champagne. Among them was Vivienne, my wife and Jim's mother. *She was a double winner for she got both of us back safe and sound.*

The radio announcers waited patiently with their tape recorders while I embraced my wife and friends and we toasted our success with champagne. They wanted our impressions of the places we had been and of how it felt to be home. Each of our

The welcoming committee with red carpets, balloons and chilled champagne.

"I dreaded the thought of saying Good Bye". Jim, Ken, Don, Tal.

answers were different for we each had seen the world slightly differently. Jim and I, after all, are a generation apart.

Tal and Ken stood by and watched. They had not yet completed their odyssey. They had yet to go on to Edmonton, Alberta for that was where THEY began. Once more we embraced, shook hands, and watched as they departed west over their final horizon.

Jim and I stood for a moment and quietly smiled at each other. As father and son we had flown around the world together, sharing the good times and bad. We had a host of new experiences and a wealth of new knowledge to reflect upon. We had remained the best of friends and yet we were glad to be home.

20

The Ultimate Challenge

REFLECTIONS

Jim and I have lived our dream. Far away exotic places are now real, vivid memories. Never again will we view the world quite the same way. We have successfully completed a trip that challenged our organizational and flying skills to the limit. We have also suffered the frustrations of continually attempting to fit a square peg into a round hole. We bet everything on the ability of my little aeroplane to do the job – and won! There is a sense of accomplishment within us but there is also a sense of smallness. The world is no longer as large as we had thought and neither are we.

This trip was unique. We didn't just fly around the world – we *visited* around the world. Every second day saw us exploring a new country with different customs. The rapid succession of countries and juxtapositiion of cultures allowed us to make comparisons and distinctions we would not normally appreciate. Comparisons were vivid, for the past was always still fresh. The kaleidoscope of lands and people that passed before our eyes will stay with us forever as Jim and I now head our separate ways. Before we parted, we took stock of the interesting things we had seen and done over the past two months.

We: Flew the Pacific, South Pacific, Indian and North Atlantic oceans.
Flew the Red, Mediterranean and South China seas.
Flew the Persian Gulf during hostilities.
Visited five of the six continents.
Visited 19 countries, Micronesia and Melanesia.
Flew over seven other countries.
Flew over icebergs and through Monsoon rains.
Crossed the International date line.
Crossed the equator twice.
Persevered through frustrating mechanical breakdowns in Oakland.
Toured an active Nuclear submarine.
"Flew" a Japanese Zero sitting ninety feet underwater.
Saw wild Wallabies "down and under," in Australia.
Watched colorful Balinese Dancers perform.
Swam at a topless beach in Bali.
Drank an original Singapore Sling in the famous Raffles Hotel.
Saw the Palace of "The King and I" fame in Bangkok.
Sat at the feet of the Emerald Buddha, in Thailand.
Rode a Long Boat down the Chao Phraya River in Bangkok.
Went back in time over forty years during a visit to Burma.
Watched public cremations beside the Bhagmati River in Nepal.
Flew alongside the Himalayas and over the Alps and Rocky mountains.
Visited the Taj Mahal in India.
Landed in the desert of Saudi Arabia.
Visited the tomb of King Tut in Luxor, Egypt.
Rode a camel around The Great Pyramids of Giza, Cairo.
Visited the League of Nations in Geneva, Switzerland.
Overnighted in The Land of the Midnight Sun, Iceland.
Flew more than 26,000 miles, mostly over water.
Brought home our liferaft, life–preservers and survival kits unused.

We had been helped and hindered along the way in approx–imately equal proportions. We never felt, however, that we were in any danger from the people or the authorities. Good fortune saw to it that both aircraft functioned well when it really counted and in places where service was unobtainable. Our health was sustained throughout the adventure. The risks we took were mainly in the air, although there were times when I felt that we gambled as much by riding in some of the Third World taxis.

As I reflect on the trip a year later, I feel very lucky. My life has been enriched beyond all measure by the sights I saw and the people I met as I circled this fascinating world of ours. I only wish there had been room to have the rest of my family along to share these experiences with us. When I recall the poverty and destitution that less fortunate human beings are forced to endure, I thank my lucky stars that I was privileged to be born and brought up on this greatest of all continents, North America!

I am often asked what my next challenge is likely to be. I may be a little old for it now, but there is one horizon left that I would still like to challenge – *"I wonder what the age limit is for astronauts?"*

Thank you for flying FONGAIR.